The
Fairy
Elephant
Effect

Elysabeth Wolter

Publisher: Elysabeth Wolter
© Elysabeth Wolter 2024
The copyright of this book, including all content within, is held by the author and all rights are reserved.
ISBN 978-0-473-72351-4
Front cover: Artwork by Elysabeth Wolter

From someone who was told that they could not have any children at 16 and then to have the three of you.

I may not have always got it right.

But having you was always right.

To Luke, Micheal, and Danielle

And to Louise

Perfect timing, Perfect person

Elysabeth Wolter

Elysabeth Wolter is a multi-talented artist, certified EFT (Emotional Freedom Techniques) practitioner, and life coach who guides individuals from a state of surviving to thriving. Originally from Gisborne and now based in Whanganui, New Zealand, she draws on a rich background in emotional healing and personal development. Elysabeth holds diplomas in counselling, psychology, art, and NLP (Neuro-Linguistic Programming), equipping her with a diverse skill set to help others overcome emotional barriers and achieve lasting transformation.

Her work focuses on empowering individuals to release limiting beliefs and cultivate resilience through practical techniques like EFT tapping. Elysabeth leads "TURN the TIDE with Tapping," a free Facebook community dedicated to helping members overcome stress and emotional challenges. She also runs programs such as the "Dream Catchers and Cultivators Club," where participants are inspired to align their lives with their values and passions.

As an author, Elysabeth shares her insights and personal experiences in books like The Fairy Elephant Effect, which offering readers practical tools for growth and healing. Her mission is to support others in breaking free from survival mode, embracing their true potential, and living a life of fulfillment and joy through art, coaching, and transformative practices.

Contents

Prologue 9
The Fairy Elephant Effect 11
Breaking Free 13
To Dance or Not to Dance 14
Beneath the Surface 17
From Comparison to Connection 20
Rising from the Muddy Hole 32
The Courage to Choose Yourself 42
Codependence 49
Letting go of the Fairytale 58
A Turning Point – Tiniroto 65
Elements and Finding Joy Beyond Trauma 68
The Illusion of Powerlessness 78
Cups 83
Discovering Self-Worth and Your Love Language 120
The Unseen Ripples of Rejection 134
Breadcrumbs and New Destinations 138
Unveiling the Layers of Self 140
The Power of Language 145
EFT Tapping: A Path to Freedom 159
Way Back Then 173
Fight, Flight, Freeze and Fawn 181
Hiccups Along the Way 186
Igniting Your Own Fire 197

Prologue

What is the Fairy Elephant Effect?

I had a friend stay the night recently, and in the morning, she was getting ready to head off, and she put this gorgeous multi-coloured horizontal dress on.

I commented that she looked very nice and was in the right colourway for our membership group, too.

She replied. "Well, are you sure because, years ago, when my daughter was nearly two years old, I took my daughter to preschool. I vividly remember that the head teacher came over to me and said, "' I don't mean to tell you how to dress your child – but you cannot put her in horizontal stripes as it just makes her look bigger than she already is.'"

"She was quite chubby at that point. And I didn't react like I would now – I just took that as, oh, I should have known that – how did I not know that and felt really embarrassed."

"I never put her in horizontal stripes again. And now, years later, while putting this dress on myself, I wonder if it makes me look bigger than I am. I have put on a little more weight." And she indicated her tummy.

I assured her that she looked amazing.

Because the thing is, my friend has an amazing, gorgeous, slim, womanly body.

But that is the Fairy Elephant Effect Because people have said and done things that sit in that place in us that gives us the impression that we are broken, faulty, unworthy, useless, unteachable, unintelligent, ugly, fat, too thin to 'do that' and we're never enough. These interactions create a plonk in our ponds, and as we collect those things, our ponds get clogged up and dry up, as we often feel our lives are.

That's a pebble/stone/rock in your pond instead of a ripple in the pond where we get to be who we are and we're delicious and amazing and we're here for a reason and we are enough!

And you know, when we are able to tune in ourselves and have a relationship that supports the growth and belief that we are enough, and more than enough, we become not only the authentic but magnificent people we were supposed to be. Our ponds have the ability to create ripples that affect the whole world. And we get to decide how big that world is going to be for us.

The Fairy Elephant Effect

People, incidences, narratives, and events that had put stones into our ponds. So many stones, sometimes little pebbles, sometimes big stones, sometimes rocks, sometimes even a boulder or two, so that there is very little water left in our ponds. It is muddy and has very little flow (much like how our lives can feel) and we are stuck – stuck with all of those negative life-draining thoughts and beliefs we have taken on as absolute truths so that we fit in and are likable and perhaps loveable.

It is nearly criminal that we carry all these stories about ourselves, and it is a wonder we are able to live functionally at all, having to jump and accommodate all those hoops to just be accepted. And acceptance could be minimal. A scrap, even.

It makes our world smaller and scarier as we don't have any trust in our own ability, voice or thoughts to make decisions, let alone deserve to have a good life. And, of course, it relates to how we feel about ourselves. We become the first to criticize and negate anything that could shift us out of this small, lifeless pond with its limited thinking and beliefs.

Does this connect with you?

Do you have a story of The Fairy Elephant Effect in your life?

We all have them, and often more than one.

That sense of impending doom – the waiting and expecting some sort of reprimand or ridicule for being you, for daring to laugh, talk, or express ourselves in a way that could be seen as naughty. Bad, waste of space. Annoying and so on and so on – anything that was negative that fell out our parents', teachers', or siblings' mouths, depending on their feelings at the time about us and their own worldview.

So welcome to the Fairy Elephant Effect book, in here we are going to look at those stories and accept them as part of the story till now.

And THEN we are going to clean out the pond and create ripples out into the world from a place of self-love, self-acceptance, and self-activation.

You see, what I have found out about me is that I was never broken. I had just a lot of FAIRY Elephant moments that stopped me from seeing and caring about me – the person who always wanted to be heard and couldn't get a look in.

Come along and discover you – the magical you, the clever you, the brilliant, the gorgeous you, the worthy you, the person you like and love in the mirror you.

Because you are the most important person in the room. It starts and finishes with you.

YOU MATTER – absolutely!

So please join me in this exploration of self-discovery, empowerment, and acceptance of you in a delicious and authentic way, and in the book, there will be opportunities for you to actively engage in the self-directed tasks at the end of each chapter.

Let this book be your companion, guiding you toward a more purposeful, fulfilling, and empowered life free to move forward with the knowledge that you are more than OK you are needed.

"The freedom from something is not true freedom. The freedom to do anything you want to do is also not the freedom I am talking about. My vision of freedom is to be yourself." — Osho

Breaking Free

Why share my story? Maybe because I believe that "all boats rise on the tide." We all come from somewhere, and in those places, we experience both good and not-so-good things. For me, there were difficult aspects of my family dynamic as well as personal incidents with my father that profoundly shaped my journey. In 2003, I was diagnosed with complex post-traumatic stress disorder (C-PTSD), and I struggled with severe anxiety, phobias, and overwhelmingly negative thoughts. At times, I was suicidal, finding it hard to stand up under the weight of it all. I lived a hyper-vigilant life, constantly anticipating the next bad thing.

As a child, anything new felt terrifying because, in my world, new didn't mean good. The emotional imprint of my experiences—both within my family and with my father—stayed with me and colored every aspect of my life. That fear, the need to be on guard, and the weight of those early experiences shaped how I moved through the world.

In my story, you might find pieces that reflect your own life, or perhaps help you understand someone close to you. That's why I'm sharing it. I firmly believe that when one person begins the healing journey, they create a ripple effect, helping others see the path more clearly. When we rise, we can help those around us rise, too.

Healing is possible. On the other side of all the pain, the torment, and the feeling of being stuck, there is a life of freedom. I've worked hard to live freely in myself, and I'm here to tell you that it's possible for you, too. It's time to step out of the puddles and past the stones that have held us down.

Let's rise.

To Dance or Not to Dance

1 so wanted to do ballet, but my mother told me I was a Fairy Elephant; my mother told me other things like I wish I had never had you; I wish you had never been born. You are too noisy. You can't sit still. You are annoying me; what is the matter with you?

Can't you listen, can't you be good? I can't take you anywhere.

You are so naughty and so on ... some of the Fairy Elephant Effects I have been able to ignore much faster than some of the others. Those others took longer to be relegated to having no importance in my life.

I had a friend at primary school who went to ballet classes; I was envious as it wasn't just the dancing and the twirling, but her mum seemed interested and went with her. It was a big thing, and my friend seemed important in her family and treated well. Special. Perhaps even wanted.

It did bother me about the dancing as I wanted to dance. I loved dancing – loved moving, I never sat still. I probably would have been diagnosed as having ADHD these days. I was curious about everything and always wanted to make people happy as I perhaps thought if others were happy, it would fall on me, too. That happiness thing.

Dance is still a part of my life now and has been present in many forms throughout my life.

The next dancing incident was when I was around eight or nine. After the house was cleaned from top to bottom every Saturday morning, we were all kicked outside for the rest of the day (In winter, it was the hall or our rooms.). The green cup would be put by the outside tap, and lunch would, 95% of the time, be sandwiches, either marmite, marmite and lettuce, or super lucky us, marmite and cheese. This particular day, my parents had visitors, and outside were their kids and several kids from down the street, too, plus some of my siblings.

We had a new thing, a table, a round wooden one, that was left over from laying cable, and I wanted to show off my dancing skills. Telling anyone who would listen that I was a ballerina.

Here I was on the top, talking loudly, OK, shouting to get everyone's attention. I stood up on my tippy toes and twirled. It felt wonderful, and as I moved my legs, the rest of my body didn't really move with them, and the grace I had anticipated just didn't happen. What did happen was I heard a new sound from my body, and I felt the snap.

The only thing that had moved was my right leg; it had twirled itself around my left leg and snapped. If I had had those dance lessons, well, that is all I will say about that.

It took me nearly six hours to convince my parents something was wrong with my leg. I was in plaster for six weeks.

Years later, when I was married and the kids were still young, I went with a friend from high school to adult ballet classes.

They really were good; each week, we would go learn plies, pirouettes, barre, and jete. The jete was the graceful running and lifting into the air across the room. So beautiful!

Each week the tutor would suggest that I relax a bit more to get into the flow. Because flow I did not. Getting to these classes, I had to jump through so many hoops, but I was determined to go. My husband expected the house spotless, all the toys away, dinner made, kids fed, and the youngest in bed.

He did not believe in babysitting – I will leave you to come to any conclusions about that. He made it nearly impossible for me to go to the class some evenings.

When running across the floor jumping, with legs in a split sort of angle – I was unable to get the positioning right and landing was always with a very pronounced thump. The pirouettes were a nightmare too, as I was constantly dizzy.

Everyone around me seemed to have some grace or poise, but it wasn't available to me in either my body or mind. But I loved being able to move.

My chance to be a ballet dancer was long gone.

Perhaps it is because my mother told me I was a FAIRY ELEPHANT.

And perhaps because I believed her.

It was a definite, no – what are you thinking? – you, do ballet? – Laughable, and don't annoy me – at the same time.

We all have stories where we have experienced the Fairy Elephant Effect.

"It's never too late to have a happy childhood."
— Tom Robbins

Beneath the Surface

Early on, after my parents separated, my mother had been a Catholic but was shunned from the church when she divorced my father. This was before we found out that my father had been married in the Netherlands before he immigrated to New Zealand.) He said he had never been married before and married my mother at 17, pregnant, in the Catholic church.

It was a big thing when we found out, which was around 1972 when his supposed son started to write to my father. My father denied it, and at that time, we didn't know if he had divorced his first wife. The shame and embarrassment for my mother must have been tremendous (and I do have a brother in the Netherlands named Huub. This was confirmed about three years ago). As if his cheating for 24 years out of a 25-year marriage, all the lies that went with it, wasn't enough.

I vividly remember when my parents were still together, the day my then-called Uncle Case arrived at dinner time one evening. Here were all of us, maybe not my elder brother Ross, but the other five of us and my mother. We could all see the back door where Uncle Case was standing facing towards my father who had his back to us. And we could all hear them; my younger siblings might not have understood the conversation, but they definitely felt the tension in the air.

Here was a man confronting my father and asking if he was having an affair with his wife. My father was an actor without ever being on stage. He threw his arms in the air and wailed, yes, wailed, saying, "How could you think that? You are my best friend; I would never do that to you or anything like that." Then came the tears.

Uncle Case left, and we never saw him again. Several years later, when my mother filed for divorce, she had to have a good reason, and part of her case was his affair with Uncle Case's wife.

There was the whole court thing, and I had to get up and testify as well. I was privy to a lot of information about what had happened in my parent's marriage. Being the oldest girl at home since my parents separated, I had this huge responsibility put on me of caring for my younger siblings and helping out significantly to keep the house.

I am dyslexic (there are places in the world now that only hire people who are Dyslexic, especially in creative industries). But at school, I was called lazy, talked too much, stupid, and didn't pay attention. It is funny because I love learning and am a lifelong learner-they the teachers just did not know how to communicate with me. I can still see that classroom at my primary school, and the teacher humiliating me for not being able to spell and not being able to pronounce words properly.

I had wanted to shrink under the floor. I started scribbling so no one could read my writing, and I kept hiding it for years. Now it would be nice to go back and read what I wrote occasionally. OK, I can write nicely sometimes and can be understood but certainly not in morning pages (you will learn about these later).

You know my mother turned up when I was in high school and studied English and Māori, in which she received a high UE mark (year 12 now). I sat School C English twice and failed at 47% both times. My grammar and spelling were counted as a lot of my failed marks – it was another slap in the face for me. My mother had never – my whole life helped me with homework. So, she may or must have thought I was useless. The thing was, I loved home economics and excelled in it. I won a school award as the top student in Home Economics. I went up on stage and was so proud and happy for myself.

No one else was proud or happy for me.

When I told my mother my dream of being a home economics teacher and going to Dunedin to study, there wasn't even a second before the answer came. My mother was sitting on the heater, her all-year seat even in summer, outside her room in the kitchen. I was by the bench at the end of the table. If there had been some hesitation or recognition, I may have felt better. But no.

"You have to stay here and look after your sister and brother."

I don't remember if she even looked at me when I said it.

End of conversation ...

Tick! Another Fairy Elephant Effect achieved.

From Comparison to Connection

"Change will not come if we wait for some other person or some other time. We are the ones we've been waiting for. We are the change that we seek." —Barack Obama

When my parents separated, I was in my first year of intermediate school—the year I also became a woman. It was a time of immense change and overwhelming emotions. Life had always been strict, with many conditions in place, and my mother was the enforcer of those rules. But after the separation, things shifted even more. Our household was still very traditional, and because of my mother's own story—she had been the oldest girl in her family—there was this unspoken expectation that I would take on more responsibility around the house. I was expected to help care for my younger siblings and do more of the household chores.

It wasn't just the physical workload that changed, though. I was drawn into the emotional dynamics of my parents' separation. Whenever my father would call, I would have to sit next to the phone and listen to him hurl abusive words at my mother. I also had my first encounter with someone who was drunk—my Uncle Peter—who came to our house, and I found myself standing as a buffer to his aggression and unwanted attention towards my mother.

My relationship with my mother also transformed during this time. Instead of just being a child she seemed distant from, I became the person she relied on when she wasn't feeling well, whether she was suffering from anxiety or some illness. In those moments my mother felt closer to me; she was actually kinder, and it was confusing to experience. But as soon as she got better, she would revert back to that colder, distant person I knew before. It was a strange dynamic—this temporary tenderness that would vanish the moment she regained her strength.

Every Saturday morning in our house was dedicated to spring cleaning, no matter the season. Everyone was expected to help—each bedroom was thoroughly cleaned, sheets stripped and washed, and even the fireplace would be scrubbed, regardless of whether it was summer. Dusting was done, and by mid-morning, we would stop for lunch. Sometimes we had a couple of biscuits as a treat.

But the work didn't stop after lunch. Once a month on a Saturday afternoon meant more chores. We would be assigned tasks like cleaning all the windows of our large house, scrubbing the bottoms of pots under the shade of a tree, polishing the copper, or doing the ironing. Playing down the street was rare—there was always work to be done.

One of the chores I dreaded most was cleaning the windows. I struggled to get them spotless, and my mother would always inspect my work; I wasn't done until it reached her standard. One afternoon, after hours of effort and growing frustration, I was desperate to finish and go play. But when she came out once more to say it still wasn't right, something snapped. In a surge of anger and hopelessness, I punched the window, shattering the glass. Of course, I didn't get to go and play—instead, it earned me a hiding. This happened before my parents split up, so I was less than 11.5 years old. And honestly, I'm still not that good at windows, but who really cares?

During the week, the routine was just as regimented. From the age of five, we were responsible for making our own beds and packing our own lunches. After breakfast, we would wash and dry the dishes, take out the rubbish, sweep the kitchen floor, and clean the bathroom and toilet. My mother's bedroom, which was off the kitchen, would remain locked, and she wouldn't get up until after we had left for school. Despite her absence in the mornings, we knew we had to complete those chores.

After school, there were even more tasks waiting for us. I often had to catch the bus into town to pay bills for my mother or pick up groceries. My mother didn't learn to drive until after my parents separated, which I always found intriguing, considering she had six kids and a husband who was frequently away as a traveling salesman. I have no concrete evidence, but it always felt as though my father didn't want her to have too much independence. Perhaps he wanted to control her movements, knowing where she was at all times by keeping her reliant on others for transportation.

Back in those days, my mother had another ritual—Sunday was gardening day. Now, as an adult, I love gardening, but as a child, it was pure torture. We would start the day with church—yes, my parents would go together, and we'd attend Catholic Mass in the morning. But the afternoon was reserved for hours of working in the garden, which I absolutely despised. So, I would slip away across the road to the Bothamleys' house. They had such a free and easygoing household where they could do whatever they wanted. I would gorge myself on food there because they didn't ration like we did at home.

Coming home, however, was a different story. Just outside our back door, there was a porch with two doors—one led to the washhouse, and the other to the kitchen. As soon as you walked through the door, on your right was the hot water cupboard. And it was in that cupboard where my mother kept the cane. If I had been caught avoiding the garden or disobeying in some way, she would wait for me there, cane in hand. She would corner me, and then, with nowhere to escape, she would beat me with it. Afterwards, I would often be sent to bed without dinner. This routine happened nearly every Sunday because, in my defiance, I would purposely stay away, fueling my rebellion by eating beforehand at the Bothamleys'.

Among my siblings, I was different. While my brothers and sisters had their own personalities, I always seemed to be the one pushing boundaries. I've heard stories from old neighbors that when I was just 18 months old, my mother would tie me to the clothesline because I had a habit of trying to run down the road. Even at that age, if I didn't stay put, I would get a smack or a hiding. I often wonder why they didn't just put up a gate at the end of the driveway—it seems like it would've saved everyone a lot of trouble.

But now, looking back, I understand that some of the harsh discipline we experienced had little to do with us as children. It was more about our parents—about their need for control in a life that often felt out of their hands. Their strictness and punishments were likely their way of asserting some order and power in a world that, for them, must have often felt chaotic and uncontrollable.

As a young girl, around 11, 12, or 13, I found myself with an overwhelming amount of responsibility that caused a lot of friction between me and my siblings. I had this power over them—power that wasn't appropriate for someone my age—but I had it, and I wielded it. My younger sister and brother had to deal with me acting like I was all-powerful. I had this sense of authority, almost like I had been granted permission to be in charge. And I can't say I was always nice about it. I mirrored a lot of my mother's behaviors, probably because I was desperate for her to see me, to recognize me, to love me. I wanted to hear her say, "You're amazing, Elysabeth. You're doing such a good job. I'm so proud of you for helping me." But, of course, she never said those things.

The only time my mother ever expressed any softness was when she was struggling—when she was anxious, sick, or overwhelmed by her own internal battles. My mother was a lot to handle, I suppose because her escape was sinking into a sea of negative thoughts. But even then, her approval or affection was fleeting, conditional.

My older siblings didn't come around much—my older brother only once, and my older sister never returned. To them, I was just annoying, even more so than when we were younger and all still together. And it's true—I've always had a strong sense of justice, honesty, and openness. I've always wanted to have real conversations, to get to the truth of things. But in a family environment where everyone was just surviving, where we all hid things, there wasn't space for real, meaningful connections.

For nearly 25 years, I had little to do with my younger brother until I made the decision, as an adult, to go and see him. We had grown up in an environment where survival came first, and there was so much pain between us. Layers and layers of it.

I think this is something many can relate to—the way we come through difficult experiences and the stories that are placed on us as children. Unless we take the time to actually examine those stories and ask ourselves if they still serve us or if they're the best way for us to be in the world now, we end up just repeating patterns.

One thing I am proud of, though, is that none of my siblings have treated their own children the way our mother treated us. Without even planning it, we all—individually—made decisions to create different relationships with our children, to rewrite that painful pattern. We've broken that cycle.

As a single parent, navigating fear and raising three kids with the youngest just 15 months and the oldest nearly 7, I haven't always gotten it right. But I've always believed in my children and that they would grow up to be remarkable people. There were times when chaos was swirling around us, and I had to work through some intense narratives—

things I carried from my own past. Even when life was overwhelming and I could no longer keep it all bottled up, I tried to soldier on because we do that, don't we? We keep pushing forward, wanting everyone to think we're okay, even when we're not.

I don't know about you, but when I was younger, anxiety would follow me everywhere. I'd go somewhere, filled with panic, sweating through every inch of me, convinced people were staring at me, judging me—whether it was because I wasn't wearing the right clothes, wasn't thin enough, or wasn't saying the right things. My head would spin with self-doubt: I'm not good enough. And then, of course, I'd look at someone else and think they had it all figured out—the right clothes, the perfect smile, looking happy and confident.

But you know what? I've learned that most of them were just playing the game, just like I was. It turned out far fewer people had it together than I had imagined. This is the danger of comparison—it's a killer. When we compare ourselves to others, we'll never measure up. We're using someone else's ruler to judge our lives, our worth, our success. It's exhausting, and in the end, it's impossible to win.

I don't do that anymore. Now, I focus on building a relationship with myself from the inside out. I check in with myself daily.

I ask, Hey, Elysabeth, how are you feeling today?

Is this the best decision for you?

And let me tell you, this practice has changed my life.

So, I'd like to introduce you to a couple of things that can help you stop looking outward for validation and instead connect with your inner self. It's time to throw away that old, external ruler. You are amazing, even if you don't always believe it. Just because you might not see it doesn't mean it isn't true. You'd be surprised others might be looking at you and thinking, Wow, you seem to have got it together. I've heard it before myself when I finally had the courage to say I wasn't feeling great. People were shocked because they thought I had it all figured out.

We're all conditioned to make things appear right, even when they're not. But it's time to break that conditioning, connect deeply with ourselves, and embrace who we truly are. You are enough, just as you are.

So, here are two powerful exercises to help you stop looking outward for validation and instead connect with your inner self. It's time to break that old conditioning and embrace the amazing person you truly are.

The "I Finally Get To..."

This exercise will help you tap into your inner desires and uncover what's been waiting to be expressed. Here's how it works:

Grab a Piece of Paper: This isn't about overthinking. This is about quickly letting out what's inside of you. So, find some quiet time and space, even if it's just 20 minutes in your car or at home.

Write "I Finally Get To..." Repeatedly: Write down "I finally get to..." and keep completing that sentence. Don't censor or analyze—just let it flow. For example: "I finally get to have that holiday," "I finally get to feel good about my body," "I finally get to like who I am."

Write 20 to 40 Statements: Aim for a minimum of 20, but 30 to 40 statements would be even better. Remember, this is a fast-paced exercise—no pondering for minutes. The goal is to let your subconscious guide you.

Reflect: Once you've finished, go back and read your list. You'll be surprised by what comes up. You'll find things like, "I finally get to feel good about my life," or "I finally get to pursue my passion." These are powerful insights coming from within.

Create a New List: Take the most resonant items from your "I Finally Get To" list and write them on a new list. These are the desires your inner self has been waiting to express. You'll be amazed by the wisdom you uncover.

"You don't have to be great to start, but you have to start to be great. Give it a go and see where it takes you." —Zig Ziglar

Priming your day with love and direction

Starting your day with a positive mindset can set the tone for a successful and fulfilling day. This guide will walk you through a detailed morning priming routine to help you connect with your body, express gratitude, and align your intentions with your life's purpose. Feel free to customize this routine with specific goals or intentions for your day.

This starts us with connecting to our lifelong companion-our body. The first place of connection is going to be there.

Connecting with Your Body

While in bed, before you get up: you lie comfortably with your back straight, take a few deep breaths to relax.

This technique may help:

Box breathing is a deep breathing technique that activates your parasympathetic nervous system, which helps calm you down.

Inhale for 4 seconds.

Hold your breath for 4 seconds.

Exhale for 4 seconds.

Hold your breath for another 4 seconds.

This technique is also very useful if you are feeling overwhelmed or anxious to reset your nervous system and create mental space for clear thinking. It can also stop worry in its tracks, by focusing your mind.

Gently place both of your hands over your heart area, just above your chest.

Start by expressing gratitude and say the following affirmations out loud or in your head, feeling their significance:

"I am so grateful for my body."

"I love and appreciate my body."

"My body is amazing."

Focus on Specific Needs: If there are specific areas in your body that need attention(pain, discomfort, or healing), address them by saying something like:

"I am so pleased that my [specific area] is feeling better."

"I am thankful for the improvements in my [specific area]."

Feel the Connection: Take a moment to feel the connection between your hands, your heart, and the positive affirmations you've expressed.

Expressing Gratitude and Setting Intentions

Reflect on Your Life and Relationships: Close your eyes and spend a moment thinking about your life and the people you share it with.

Express Gratitude for Your Life: Say out loud or in your mind:

"I am so grateful for my life and the people I get to share it with."

Send Positive Energy: Focus on the people who come to your mind and send them good energy and well wishes.

Set Intentions for the Day

Affirm your intentions for the day by saying things like:

"Today, may I be the best version of myself."

"I am aligned with my soul's purpose."

"May I take inspired actions that lead me to the

right places for me and/or my business."

"Thank you that I can help others today."

"My intention for today is ...."

Acknowledge and express gratitude for the specific opportunities or challenges you anticipate for the day by adding:

"Thank you for the opportunities to ...."

Take a moment to reflect on Living Your Best Life

Conclude your morning priming routine by saying:

"Thank you that I am living my best life."

"Thank you, thank you."

The key is to start your day with a positive mindset, gratitude, and a clear sense of purpose.

Every insight and moment of reflection is a step toward your greater truth.

You're doing beautifully.

Fairy Elephant Effect

Growing up, my mother always told me and my siblings that she was the ugly one. It wasn't just something she thought—it was something her family had drilled into her, comparing her to her sister, who they deemed the beautiful one. Even though my mother was so talented, and far from ugly, those words stuck with her for her entire life. She believed it, and because she believed it, I did too.

When people would tell me I looked just like my mother, I didn't hear it as a compliment. Instead, I heard, "You must be ugly too," because that was how she had always spoken about herself. For a long time that became my story. I carried that belief with me, thinking that if I looked like her, I must not be attractive.

But that's not my story anymore. It's taken time, but I've come to realize that what others said about my mother didn't define her—and it certainly doesn't define me. She was beautiful in her own right, and so am I. I've learned to see myself differently, to break free from that limiting belief, and embrace who I am without those old, hurtful labels.

J.W

Rising from the Muddy Hole

"Change is painful, but nothing is as painful as staying stuck somewhere you don't belong." — Mandy Hale

As you read this book, I encourage you to reflect on your own experiences. Think about the moments when you've felt a deeper sense of knowing, a connection to something greater than yourself. These moments are your higher consciousness guiding you. They are reminders that you are capable of more than you realize.

It's time to start living your life on your terms. It's time to let go of the past and embrace the possibilities of the future. Remember, you are the author of your own story. You have the power to create a life that is fulfilling and joyful. So, start where you are and take that first step toward a new beginning. You matter, and your journey matters. Let's make it a journey worth taking.

When I sit down to think about the situations I've been in and the people who have come and gone from my life, sometimes it feels overwhelming. It's as if another person entirely lived those experiences; that's how far removed I am now from the other versions of Elysabeth. From childhood, I still remember certain memories, ones that seem important in some way, but there were many years of complete nothingness—of things I don't recall at all. The memories that have resurfaced are those tied to strong emotions.

In the case of abuse, though, my memory is selective—a way to protect myself from things that were incomprehensible to a young child and, to be honest, are still incomprehensible to me as an adult. There was always a sense, a knowing, that something was wrong, but

I wasn't able to articulate that feeling. Growing up, and for many others as well, what happened at home stayed at home. It was a punishable offense to speak about it. The repercussions were serious, and the entire society operated under that unspoken code.

When I was around 15, my mother beat me with a kettle cord. I had hundreds of welts across my body. I distinctly remember not crying during that beating—it felt like a victory, a small act of defiance against her. I told myself it would be the last time she'd ever hit me.

Let me put that into perspective: I was raised by a mother who ran a tight ship. If I didn't end a conversation with "yes, mum" or "no, mum," I'd get slapped, or something would be taken away from me—whatever would hurt the most at that moment. So, I followed the rules. You didn't talk back, you didn't roll your eyes, and you didn't fail to answer correctly. Nearly everyone brought up in that environment struggles to let go of it, let alone stand up and make a different decision because the power dynamic was so deeply ingrained.

The day you leave home is the day you long for, but that narrative—the stories and beliefs about yourself—comes with you. Out in the world, you find yourself feeling more unsafe than ever before. You're in a hard place, or perhaps no place at all. You might feel ruined, attracting more of the same story because it's the only one you know.

The societal pull, the need to fit in, was strong. My mother's temper had flared because I'd run away for the weekend—an act of defiance. I knew I'd be in trouble, but I didn't expect it to be that bad. I had run away before to escape the housework, but this time it was different because other girls were involved. Their mothers called mine, and that triggered my mother's shame and embarrassment. It was never really about me; it was always about what the neighbors would think.

That same pressure played out with my older brother, the one just a little older than me and my mother's favorite. He was in the 6th form (year 12), had no problems with school, and had recently passed his University Entrance exam. One night, he and his mates had a drink, and when they dropped him home, they were a bit loud and broke a couple of bottles outside. My mother was furious. She got a softball bat out of the hall cupboard and took it to his head in the hallway, it was a long way up there for her. My brother was the tallest in the family being over 6 feet 3 inches..

She was so embarrassed by his behavior and the complaints from the neighbors. He didn't dare say anything or fight back.

The Fairy Elephant Effect

As a young child, J.M. constantly felt like nothing she did was ever right in her mother's eyes. After yet another argument that blurred into many others, her mother marched her down the hallway and pointed to an old photo, accusing her of being as angry as the woman in the faded, oval-framed picture. It was a distant relative, but the image would come to haunt J.M. for years. From that moment on, every time she looked at the picture, it wasn't just the stranger in the photo she saw—it was her own reflection, the "angry" child of the family.

Her older brother and younger sister, both with blonde hair and seemingly perfect in every way, only deepened her belief that she was less than, always overshadowed. The weight of this perception followed her into adulthood, creating barriers with men and stifling her self-confidence. She carried the belief that no one could truly love her because she was "angry."

But as years passed, J.M. began to understand that the reflection in the photo wasn't hers. It was a projection of her mother's frustration and pain. She embarked on a journey of healing, where she finally learned to love the person she saw in the mirror— her true, beautiful self, not the angry child she once believed she was.

J.M.

Individually, my siblings and I have chosen to treat our children differently. We broke that cycle. I can't say I was perfect, and in the early days of parenting, I wasn't as considerate as I would have liked, but I never spoke into my children's lives the way my mother had done to me. I did my best until I learned better ways to be my best.

I'm certain that the way my life unfolded was connected to the societal narrative of the time—where the man was the head of the household, and everyone had to live under his rule, whatever that might have meant to him. I've heard horror stories where children and wives endured terrible living conditions. These things were often suspected, with partial information floating around, but the "don't speak about it" rule was firmly in place. Sometimes, men knew what was happening but did nothing, blaming the wife or children, asserting that it was a man's right to behave that way.

There was a policeman on our street, and later, it came out that he beat his wife. People knew, but nothing was done.

Because we didn't talk about "things," you might have been mistaken in thinking that's how everyone lived. If you went somewhere, you were under the illusion that the same things were happening there too—or worse. For me, that was terrifying. I avoided new situations at all costs, too scared to even consider the possibilities. You never knew if one of your friend's fathers might be yelling at her or someone else in their home or worse. It was easy to spin out, to panic about what had happened or what might happen next.

As children, we were sheltered and silenced in many ways. But now we can speak up, and we have the contrast and the evidence to start making new decisions. As a kid, it was a difficult place to navigate because I never knew from one day to the next what would happen. Home was a scary place. I certainly didn't feel loved, and I had plenty of evidence that I wasn't even liked.

There are stories about my mother tying me to the clothesline because I would run down the road. I never understood why they didn't just put up a gate. Maybe punishing me was their way of relieving their inner pain. Even my older siblings found me annoying because I liked to talk. I wanted to be included. They would lock me in my room until our parents came home, and I would tell on them, thinking that if I did the right thing, someone would acknowledge me. I thought someone would say, "Well done, Elysabeth." But that never happened.

Trying to be right all the time, trying to be a good girl, didn't bring me any joy or connection. I was trying so hard to be seen, to be heard, to be loved. And, after all, any attention is better than none, right?

A New Perspective

It can feel like a stretch to imagine a different life when you're caught in the same pattern day after day. But trust me, as someone who has been there, you can pull yourself out of that muddy, sticky hole. There were days when I felt like I was just dragging myself through life, stuck in cycles of drama that kept repeating. It felt like I was sitting in a puddle up to my neck, and that puddle eventually turned into a deep, muddy hole. But on the other side of that struggle, I learned something invaluable: I get to choose where my energy goes, and that choice shapes my life.

Energy flows where attention goes. When you focus on something, it grows and gains momentum. And what you focus on expands. So, if you like drama and stress just focus on it and it will give you more of the same.

It's like pushing a rock up a hill – you are getting nowhere fast.

How about letting it go downhill? The rock will start to roll on its own, gathering speed.

When we constantly focus on what we don't want--we get more of it. That is not only the hard way, but it also reinforces negative feelings and beliefs about ourselves. Once we decide we want better and start to focus on what we do want, then we are not going against the flow but are a part of it. This momentum carries you forward, making it easier to establish new, positive habits and thoughts. It's not about being stuck or clogged up anymore; it's about allowing your energy to flow freely, giving life to new possibilities.

Taking Responsibility

Part of this journey involves taking responsibility for your thoughts and actions. It's about saying, "I'm ready to let go of the negative beliefs I have about myself. I'm ready to release these patterns." Start by incorporating one small, positive change into your life for the next three days. At the end of those three days, add another day, and another and so on. This gradual approach helps you take control of your life without feeling overwhelmed. You're responsible for yourself and your actions, not for other people's emotions.

This doesn't mean neglecting your responsibilities, like caring for your children or ensuring your household runs smoothly. But it does mean setting boundaries and not taking on the emotional burdens of others. You are in charge of your emotions and reactions. By making small adjustments—like tweaking the course of an airplane—you can find yourself heading toward a new destination, one filled with more joy and fulfillment.

The Power of Self-Love

Start where you are because you matter. Everything begins and ends with you. This realization is for everyone.

When we start showing up for ourselves, our hearts expand, our intentions become clearer, and our world becomes brighter. We're all connected, and our personal growth ripples out to those around us.

By examining these details, you can begin to uncover the factors that contribute to your connection with your higher consciousness/God or other, and your inner wisdom.

So, as you embark on this journey through the pages of this book, keep your own experiences in mind. Allow them to shape your understanding and interpretation of the ideas presented. Trust in the guidance of your higher consciousness and embrace the limitless possibilities that await you.

It's time to start living your life on your terms. It's time to let go of the past and embrace the possibilities of the future. Remember, you are the author of your own story. You have the power to create a life that is fulfilling and joyful. So, start where you are and take that first step toward a new beginning.

You matter and your journey matters.

Let's make it a journey worth taking.

Take a few moments to reflect on this chapter.

....
....
....

Write down anything that came up.

....
....
....

By writing we are allowed to see things from a different perspective.

Activity to do every day

Morning Pages

Is an incredible tool introduced by Julia Cameron in The Artist's Way, and it's about so much more than just writing. When we write by hand, it taps into a powerful metacognitive process. By putting thoughts onto paper, we create a tangible connection between the mind and the physical world. Cameron often describes it as using our own energy—even metaphorically comparing it to blood—to connect deeply with ourselves through the page.

Writing Morning Pages becomes a personal ritual, an intimate companion that offers discovery, clarity, and connection to the self. It's a safe space where you communicate with the deeper part of you that has perhaps been waiting silently. This practice provides an opportunity for reflection, insight, and release.

The process allows for an emotional and mental pause. By writing, we create space between our thoughts and emotions, allowing us to see things differently. This simple act of putting pen to paper serves as a mental decluttering process, opening up room for the subconscious and superconscious mind to step in—something that often gets lost when our conscious mind is too cluttered.

Morning Pages is not meant to be a journal for reflection or long-term memory but rather a tool for release. You're encouraged to write three A4 pages every morning, no more, no less. This structured practice offers a way to process, let go of internal noise, and make room for genuine clarity.

It may take some effort and commitment, but the benefits are immense. Morning Pages helps you uncover what you truly think, feel, and want, moving beyond the surface chatter of daily life. And when the pages are done, toss them. They are not meant for keeping. This is an exercise in letting go, not in recording history.

If you're looking for a way to get unstuck, release inner clutter, and connect more deeply with yourself, Morning Pages is a fabulous place to start.

The Courage to Choose Yourself

"There are far better things ahead than any we leave behind." — C.S. Lewis

Have you ever found yourself wishing for something drastic to happen just so you'd have an excuse to leave a relationship? Maybe you've caught yourself thinking, "I wish they would cheat on me, spend all the money, or yell at me—then I'd have a real reason to leave."

It's a familiar internal dialogue for many. It happens because we haven't yet developed the courage to step up and say, "This doesn't work for me." Instead, we hope that something external will give us permission to escape without having to bear the guilt of looking like the "bad guy."

But why do we wait for such extreme situations?

Why do we need that external validation to make a decision that's right for us?

This mindset stems from our conditioning. Many of us growing up were taught to be the "good girl" or "good boy"—to please others, to avoid confrontation, to be agreeable. We were led to believe that our value comes from how others perceive us. And because of this, we become trapped, feeling unable to make decisions based on our inner needs, paralyzed by the fear of judgment and rejection.

Have you done this? I know I have. Years ago, I found myself in a relationship where I wasn't thriving. I wasn't becoming the best version of myself, yet I didn't have the strength to leave.

I kept waiting for something terrible to happen, some event that would force me to take action. I wasn't able to say, "This doesn't work for me, and I deserve better." I wasn't thinking about how the relationship was affecting me—or even my children—I was more concerned with how I would be judged if I chose to leave.

When we are more concerned about what others think of us than what we think of ourselves, we become stuck. And that's what happens when we rely on outside validation instead of trusting our inner voice.

It's sad, isn't it? Living a life where we feel trapped in the fear of judgment and condemnation. Yet, until we shift from living for external validation to living for ourselves, we remain stuck.

Have you lived like that? Are you still living like that? It's okay if you are. But I'm here to tell you that you don't have to stay that way. Choosing yourself is the way out.

Once you make the decision to take responsibility for your life, everything changes. You no longer wait for someone to give you an excuse to act. You stop blaming others for why your life isn't working, and you start making choices that are aligned with your true desires. Yes, it can be isolating at first, as people who were part of your old patterns may fall away. You might feel a bit lonely as you start to set boundaries and distance yourself from the drama that used to fill your days. But there's beauty in that, too—because as you respond to life rather than react to it, you start to see how good it feels to be in control of your own story.

Drama does not equate to connection. I'll say that again: Drama does not equate to connection. We often mistake the intensity of emotional highs and lows for meaningful relationships, but that's not the case. When you let go of the need for drama, you begin to experience connection in a different way—a deeper, more authentic way that isn't based on constant emotional turmoil.

You'll start to react less and respond more. You'll no longer feel the need to blame others for your circumstances. Instead, you'll take ownership of your life. You'll recognize that the love you've been seeking all along is within you, not something to be found outside of yourself.

It may feel uncomfortable at first, but that discomfort is a sign that you're growing. As you strengthen your relationship with yourself, the need for external validation fades. You'll attract new people into your life—people who are also doing their inner work, people who are working to become the best versions of themselves.

This journey isn't about filling your life with people who can take up space. It's about filling your own space with love, confidence, and self-respect. And when you do that, you'll start to attract the kind of relationships that truly nourish you—relationships built on mutual respect and shared growth, not on codependency and blame.

So, I ask you, are you ready to stop wishing for an excuse and start choosing yourself? Are you ready to take responsibility for your life and live from the inside out? It may be a bit isolating at first, but I promise you this: once you start, you'll never want to go back to living any other way.

> Here is a great exercise to help you quiet your thoughts because many people are stuck in a negative and draining loop of thoughts, plus connecting emotions, going around and around all day long in their head.
>
> It is exhausting.

> It never seems to end the amount of things and people you need to manage.
>
> As well as having to solve or attempt to solve complex and seemingly impossible problems/issues.
>
> Perhaps you are stuck in the overthinking loop, which is both a pattern and also partly guilt. Many people have picked up this belief that if we don't constantly think about our partners, our parents, our jobs, our children, and more, it shows we do not care about them, and if we stop thinking about others, they may also forget us.

Here is an exercise that will help you to interrupt that pattern and free up a lot of energy, too. It is really simple but not necessarily easy.

It is called the Albert Einstein walk.

> The Albert Einstein Walk combines mindfulness and gratitude with physical movement, creating a calming experience for mental clarity. Here's a step-by-step guide to fully engage in this practice:
>
> Find Your Space: Start by standing up and finding a comfortable, quiet area where you can walk slowly without distractions. This can be outdoors in nature, inside your home, or anywhere peaceful.
>
> Slow, Intentional Steps: Begin walking at a slow pace, focusing on each step. Notice how your feet connect with the ground and the sensation of lifting and placing each foot down. Allow your movements to be deliberate and smooth.

Gratitude Mantra: As you walk, repeat the simple phrase "Thank You" in your mind with every step. Don't attach it to anything specific; instead, let the words flow naturally, filling your thoughts. The goal is to create a sense of peaceful gratitude with each step.

Breathe Deeply: Allow your arms to swing freely at your sides and take deep, steady breaths. Inhale deeply, letting the air fill your lungs, and exhale slowly, releasing any tension. Focus on how the breathing and movement harmonize, bringing calm and clarity.

Walk for as Long as You Need: Whether it's 15 minutes or an hour, walk for as long as feels comfortable. Stay present, centered on your steps, your breath, and your gratitude mantra: "Thank You."

Reflect: After your walk, take a moment to sit or stand still. Reflect on how you feel mentally and emotionally. Did the simple act of walking and repeating "Thank You" bring any shifts in your mood, stress levels, or overall mindset?

This walk serves as a grounding practice, allowing you to focus on gratitude and presence while gently moving your body. How did the experience affect you?

The Albert Einstein Walk is beneficial for several reasons, blending physical movement, mindfulness, and gratitude to promote overall well-being. Here's a deeper look into why this practice is so effective.

Promotes Mindfulness

Walking slowly with intention helps anchor you in the present moment. By focusing on each step and repeating a simple mantra, you draw your attention away from distractions and stressors, fostering a state of mindfulness. This mindful awareness can reduce anxiety and improve emotional regulation.

Enhances Gratitude

Repeating the phrase "Thank You" during your walk cultivates a sense of gratitude. Gratitude has been shown to have numerous psychological benefits, including increased happiness, reduced stress, and improved relationships. It shifts your focus from what might be lacking to what is already present and positive in your life.

Encourages Deep Breathing

Deep breathing during the walk helps activate the parasympathetic nervous system, which promotes relaxation and reduces stress. By consciously taking deep breaths, you increase oxygen flow to your brain and body, which can enhance mental clarity and physical energy.

Increases Physical Movement

Walking is a low-impact exercise that can improve cardiovascular health, increase energy levels, and support overall physical fitness. Engaging in regular walking also helps to release endorphins, which can elevate mood and reduce feelings of stress or depression.

Fosters Calm and Clarity

The combination of slow, intentional movement and deep breathing helps calm the mind and body. By focusing on the simple gratitude mantra, you create a mental space free from overwhelming thoughts, allowing for clearer thinking and a sense of inner peace.

Supports Emotional Reflection

Taking time to reflect after your walk helps consolidate the emotional benefits gained during the practice. This reflection period allows you to notice and appreciate any shifts in your mental and emotional state, reinforcing the positive impact of the exercise.

Builds a Routine for Self-Care

Incorporating practices like the Albert Einstein Walk into your routine can help establish healthy habits for self-care. Regular mindfulness and gratitude practices contribute to long-term emotional resilience and overall well-being.

Overall, the Albert Einstein Walk offers a simple yet powerful way to integrate mindfulness, gratitude, and physical activity into your daily life, promoting both mental and physical health.

"I only went out for a walk and finally concluded to stay out till sundown, for going out, I found, was really going in."
— John Muir

After the walk, reflect on how this exercise felt.

....

....

....

Did you notice any shifts in your mental or emotional state?

....

....

....

What thoughts came up for you from this chapter?

....

....

....

Codependence

Codependency is often misunderstood, but at its core, it reflects an over-dependence on others to the extent that it impairs one's ability to lead an independent life.

This needy behavior is characterized by a lack of self-sufficiency, with individuals feeling compelled to derive their sense of identity from another person.

They are consumed by the need to please others and, in turn, often enable those they depend on. This mutually destructive dynamic allows codependency to thrive in an environment where enablers encourage or facilitate this unhealthy reliance.

A core element of codependency is the belief that one must control or be responsible for another person's emotions and well-being.

This mindset often results in enablers who inadvertently reinforce the codependent's behaviors. For the enabler, the attention they receive from supporting the codependent becomes part of the unhealthy dynamic, allowing this cycle to perpetuate itself.

Gender norms can set us up for unhealthy patterns of helping and giving, often leading to an imbalance in relationships. Let's start by examining women. The cultural expectation for women to prioritize others' needs—to be selfless, nurturing, and accommodating—can lead to unhealthy self-sacrifice.

In roles like wife, mother, or daughter, women may confuse excessive caretaking with normal nurturing. This isn't because they're inherently unwell; they're simply striving to embody the cultural ideal of the 'good woman,' even at the expense of their well-being.

Men, on the other hand, are often drawn into codependency through roles that emphasize heroism, protection, and provision.

The 'man-as-rescuer' or 'man-as-provider' roles can pull men into relationships where they feel compelled to help or rescue those who would benefit from solving their own problems.

This isn't about illness either but reflects the internalization of societal expectations that push men into roles of perpetual support, sometimes to their detriment.

Now, we're going to delve into the concept of martyrdom—where this constant helping turns into a form of self-sacrifice that alienates us from fulfilling relationships with ourselves and others. How can we interrupt this widespread societal expectation? The key lies in creating relationships built on shared visions and beliefs rather than adhering to established systems that may no longer serve us. By embracing boundaries, we can start reshaping our relationships to be more fulfilling and balanced, allowing us to step away from misery and toward mutual respect and genuine connection.

Codependents are often likened to self-sacrificing martyrs who strive to be everything to everyone, often at their own expense. This behavior is deeply ingrained in societal conditioning, where people are taught that selflessness—often to an unhealthy degree—is virtuous. The idea that one's identity is tied to how much one can give or how indispensable they are to others is often rooted in early childhood experiences and reinforced by societal norms.

One of the most defining characteristics of codependency is the lack of clear boundaries. Codependents struggle to distinguish where their responsibilities end and others' begin.

They often feel responsible for the emotions and actions of others, taking on too much and overextending themselves in the process. This inability to say 'no' and set limits allows others to take advantage of their willingness to help, leaving them feeling drained and unfulfilled.

Moreover, codependents tend to live externally, constantly seeking validation and approval from those around them. In doing so, they often lose touch with their own needs, opinions, and desires. This disconnection from the self makes it nearly impossible to form healthy relationships or live a life of true self-fulfillment. Their lives revolve around trying to control external situations and people, often in a bid to avoid the chaos they fear will ensue if they don't remain in control.

One of the greatest struggles of codependents is their tendency to overthink and ruminate on situations and people. They often believe that if they let go of control, everything will fall apart. This leads to obsessive thoughts and actions driven by a fear of failing others. It's ingrained in them to prioritize others over themselves, to the point where self-care feels like a betrayal of their upbringing.

Ultimately, codependency stifles the ability to cultivate a strong relationship with oneself. Breaking free from these patterns requires embracing self-responsibility rather than focusing on others. True healing involves recognizing that self-care, self-worth, and self-compassion are not selfish but are essential to living a balanced, healthy life. When codependents begin to take care of themselves and set boundaries, they can form deeper, more fulfilling relationships with others—built on mutual respect rather than a desperate need for validation.

The transformation from codependency to self-responsibility opens the door to a healthier, more fulfilling way of living. By reclaiming their sense of self, codependents can begin to tune into their own needs, desires, and intuition, allowing them to show up as the best versions of themselves in their relationships. This shift from neediness to wholeness creates space for deeper connections, both with oneself and with others, ultimately leading to more authentic, meaningful relationships.

In relationships, this confusion can lead to codependent behavior. For example, if your partner was upset, you might have found yourself upset, too. You would spend endless hours trying to fix their problems, believing it was your job to sort things out for them.

This pattern is a hallmark of codependency, where you feel responsible for someone else's emotional well-being in the hopes that they will love and appreciate you.

Codependency is deeply ingrained in our society. We've been taught to be "nice" at all costs, especially women. Being "nice" often means suppressing our own aspirations and feelings to fit into the expectations of others. This conditioning starts in our family units, where certain beliefs and behaviors are passed down. Boys and men face their own set of expectations, often centered around providing and conforming to societal norms.

The narrative of being "nice" often means putting others first and agreeing with them, especially if you grew up with a dictatorial figure in your life. This can lead to a life of feeling small and insignificant. However, as society shifts, we see a pendulum swing in the opposite direction, with people demanding respect and acknowledgment for their boundaries. While this shift is necessary, it can sometimes go too far. The key is to find a balance and take responsibility for our own lives.

"Once you understand that habits can change, you have the freedom and the responsibility to remake them."
– Charles Duhigg

When we overthink and worry unnecessarily, it's often because we don't trust ourselves to make wise decisions or believe that life can work for us.

Read that again.

As children, we looked to significant adults for guidance and approval. It was in this space that we could gain the confidence to try new things and start trusting our abilities and decision-making. But if your environment wasn't nurturing, that trust may not have developed as it could have.

As we grow, we must learn to trust ourselves and make our own decisions. This requires us to reflect deeply on our experiences, question our judgments, and evaluate our beliefs. Through self-reflection, we can begin to trust ourselves and our decisions.

There is a habitual way of being that often involves overthinking, worrying, and distracting ourselves. These behaviors have brought us to where we are now, but the good news is that habits are not hardwired.

It's time to explore the reasons behind these habits and how they impact our lives in ways that may not serve us. By using a variety of techniques, we can create new choices that bring more contentment and satisfaction.

Words have power.

Our thoughts are the first place of creation—emotions come next.

It's through language that we shape our lives. If you experience sadness, anxiety, or other uncomfortable emotions, they often stem from your heart space and influence your language, which in turn affects your body. How we stand, sit, walk, and talk is all influenced by our thoughts, which are simply words formed into sentences.

Sometimes, illnesses can even manifest due to the thoughts we repeatedly think and the scripts that run in the background of our minds, hidden from view because of limiting beliefs, trauma, environment, or the demands of work and family life. Emotions like shame, guilt, and embarrassment play a significant role in shaping how life impacts us.

When you attach a sentence with emotion and meaning, it affects not only you but everyone around you. If you've ever been angry and said something with intent, you know this to be true. And we often say a lot of unkind things to ourselves and others.

"This requires us to reflect deeply on our experiences, question our judgments, and evaluate our beliefs. Through self-reflection, we can begin to trust ourselves and our decisions.

It's time to explore the reasons behind these habits and how they impact our lives in ways that may not serve us. By using a variety of techniques, we can create new choices that bring more contentment and satisfaction.

It's through language that we shape our lives. If you experience sadness, anxiety, or other uncomfortable emotions, they often stem from your heart space and influence of your language, which in turn affects your body.

How we stand, sit, walk, and talk is all influenced by our thoughts, which are simply words formed into sentences. Sometimes, illnesses can even manifest due to the thoughts we repeatedly think and the scripts that run in the background of our minds, hidden from view because of limiting beliefs, trauma, environment, or the demands of work and family life.

Emotions like shame, guilt, and embarrassment play a significant role in shaping how life impacts us.

When you attach a sentence with emotion and meaning, it affects not only you but everyone around you. If you've ever been angry and said something with intent, you know this to be true. And we often say a lot of unkind things to ourselves.

Our thoughts are the first place of creation—emotions come next.

These beliefs are tied to our self-worth and the fear that we can't trust ourselves to choose the right path. We may hold onto these beliefs because we've been told—sometimes repeatedly—that we are incapable or worthless. However, it's important to remember that our beliefs do not define us. We have the power to challenge and change them.
It's vital to surround ourselves with positive influences and supportive people who encourage us to believe in ourselves.

This may mean making changes in who we spend our time with.

"We may desire change, but until we take action, it remains wishful thinking." — Elysabeth Wolter

The "monkey mind" and our language have long misled us into believing things that don't serve us. This has created a series of signals that form the habits we now carry, many of which are neither helpful nor desired. Overthinking, worrying, and allowing distractions too much space not only cause damage but also create barriers to living abundantly. These habits prevent us from feeling alive, vibrant, and trusting that life is working for us.

Changing our stories and scripts begins the process of disrupting the language we use today. This disruption will reveal the emotions behind our words, and soon, the patterns will become apparent. At this point, the opportunity to steer your life in a new direction has arrived.

Here are some familiar beliefs:

To achieve anything worthwhile, we must struggle.

No matter how hard I try, I can't have what I want.

Others are allowed that, but not me.

I cannot trust myself to make good decisions.

Who do I think I am?

It's hard to make a living or have a relationship.

I must give up parts of myself to get what I want.

Being myself is not enough.

I am a failure if I am on my own.

Did any of these statements resonate with you?

....
....
....

Did others come to mind?

....
....
....
....
....

Take a few moments to jot down your thoughts.

....
....
....
....
....

"Remember that positive self-talk is an intrinsic part of a healthy mind."— Asa Don Brown

Letting go of the Fairytale

As I delved deeper into my self-discovery, I also learned about the distinction between kindness and niceness. Being kind means being authentic and honest, even if it means saying things that may not be immediately comforting. Kindness is about caring for others on a deeper level, wanting the best for them, and sometimes challenging them to see things differently. On the other hand, being nice is often about seeking approval and avoiding conflict, even if it means being dishonest or avoiding the truth. This distinction became a crucial aspect of my personal growth and self-respect.

Reflecting on my childhood, I remembered my time at primary school as a school counselor. Even at a young age, I was naturally drawn to helping others. I chose this role over being on road patrol because I found fulfillment in comforting and supporting my peers. I would talk to students, check on them, and sometimes even escort them home if they were upset. It felt normal to me, perhaps because of my own experiences at home, and it pleased me to think I could make a difference in others' lives. However, it wasn't until my late thirties that I realized the importance of helping myself. I had been so focused on reinforcing societal narratives and playing by the rules that I hadn't noticed how much I needed to care for my own well-being.

I had lived a life dictated by external expectations—being good, nice, clever, attractive, and compliant. I believed that if I adhered to these standards, I would eventually receive the rewards I longed for. But these were just illusions, and I was stuck in a cycle of trying to prove my worth to others, all while feeling fundamentally broken. Every mistake or deviation from these standards was a mark against my character, reinforcing a negative self-image that others seemed eager to uphold.

In the end, this chapter is about breaking free from those constraints. It's about recognizing that the judgments of others are not the ultimate measure of our worth. It's about understanding that true connection and self-worth come from within, not from conforming to external expectations. This realization set the stage for the next part of my journey, where I would confront the deeper issues of codependency and learn to reclaim my power and purpose.

I had been taught to have an overwhelming sense of duty to take care of others' emotional needs. I came to believe it was my responsibility to alleviate the unhappiness, anger, stress, or any other emotion others might experience. I would jump through hoops, offer my time, money, or special gestures, and even perform tasks or chores to make others feel better. It was as if I was always on high alert, tuned into the emotional landscapes around me, constantly scanning for signs of neediness, anger, resentment, disappointment, fear, or pain—both mental and physical.

This perpetual state of heightened emotional readiness defined my existence. From the moment I woke up, I was attuned to the needs and demands of others, prioritizing their well-being above my own. My sense of self was lost in the whirlwind of attending to everyone else's whims. Anxiety wasn't just a word; it was the air I breathed, a constant companion in my quest to meet others' expectations.

Growing up, I experienced the oppressive nature of codependence firsthand. My relationship with my mother and the negative influences from my father reinforced the belief that my needs were secondary. There was an expectation that others' needs always came first, especially those of men. The societal belief that men were inherently superior, possessing greater intelligence, wisdom, and authority, was a pervasive force in my upbringing. This belief system dictated that men were always right, and their pride and ego were to be protected at all costs, often at the expense of women and children.

My experiences with my uncle further exemplified this toxic dynamic. When he would visit, drunk and intent on imposing himself on my mother, I found myself in the unenviable position of having to protect her. His aggressive and threatening behavior made it clear that my mother's consent or lack thereof was irrelevant. At that time, society did not recognize "no" as a valid response; women were expected to endure such advances, and any resistance was seen as mere play-acting or worse, an invitation.

During these encounters, I became the unwilling buffer between them, a child forced to absorb verbal abuse and hostility. I felt a twisted sense of purpose in this role, already entangled in a codependent relationship with my mother. The lack of available support or protection for her added to the isolation and shame we both felt. It was a harsh reality that as a divorcee, my mother was seen as morally inferior, and any attempts to defend herself would likely have been met with blame or pity.

My father's influence was another source of instability. A charismatic liar, he maintained a facade of innocence and charm, even as he engaged in a long-term affair with a friend's wife, plus numerous other affairs for 24 years of their 25-year marriage, with the last one having him lose his job and because of the DPB (domestic purposes benefit) becoming available, my mother was finally able to have independent financial support. His deception was so convincing that he seemed to believe his own fabrications.

When confronted, he would theatrically deny the accusations, further complicating our understanding of truth and trust. He also had no boundaries with my older sister and me. I am not going to go into any detail about that.

But for myself, it took many years to understand that sex was not love. As a teenager, I searched and behaved in ways to find that elusive love thing. If only there was a dialogue in our society that could have given me the knowledge about self-love, which has associated feelings of self-respect, self-compassion, and other self-activators of positive qualities. But, alas, I was labeled with more unworthy and destructive adjectives. Now, at least, there is information and people to tell us these things.

Growing up in this environment left deep scars. The constant instability and danger instilled in me a profound sense of inadequacy, unworthiness, and an overwhelming fear of being unlovable. Trust was a foreign concept, and the idea of forming meaningful connections seemed both terrifying and unattainable. These experiences shaped my worldview, leaving me trapped in a cycle of self-doubt and self-sabotage.

However, amidst the darkness and beyond it, there is often a way forward, a light that can help us. Healing, though challenging, is possible. It starts with acknowledging the impact of these past experiences and finding the courage to confront and release their hold.

Grieving the Fairy Tale

From a young age, many of us are led to believe in a story—the fairy tale that promises a knight in shining armor will come and save us. Save us from what, though? Our families, our circumstances, or perhaps from a life of shame or loneliness? We were told that a man would arrive and, in doing so, sweep away all the pain, worry, and difficulty. Then, together, we would live happily ever after.

This narrative is deeply embedded in our culture. From classic fairy tales like Cinderella and Sleeping Beauty to modern romantic comedies, girls are often portrayed as waiting for a man to come along and make their lives complete. The message is clear: your worth is tied to finding "the one." You'll fall in love, get married, and live out your days in bliss. This "happily ever after" syndrome can be incredibly damaging because it creates unrealistic expectations for both relationships and personal fulfillment.

The reality is far more complex. Relationships require effort, communication, and a deep understanding of self. Yet, growing up, we weren't told these things. Instead, the focus was often on finding a partner who would "complete" us, as if we were not whole on our own. This left many of us unprepared for the realities of adult relationships. The fairy tale doesn't include chapters on self-responsibility, emotional labor, or personal growth. It skips over the part where we learn to communicate effectively, manage our finances, or develop the resilience needed to navigate life's challenges.

I grew up, like millions of other girls, believing that when "the one" came, life would finally start to make sense. Everything would be fixed—love, honor, and devotion would be bestowed upon me, and my needs would be fulfilled effortlessly. He would take care of the money, the house, and the burdens, while I would nurture the home and children. But as we know now, life doesn't work like that. Modern relationships require shared responsibility, open communication, and mutual respect. Both partners must contribute—not just financially but emotionally.

When my marriage ended—the relationship in which I had my children—I felt a deep sense of failure. The fairytale was over, and it felt like I had failed, not just the relationship but myself. I grieved, not just for the relationship, but for the loss of the dream I had held onto for so long. The grief wasn't just over the marriage; it was over the shattered illusion of what life was supposed to be. I felt worthless, incapable, and deeply unworthy. I had believed the fairy tale, and when it broke, so did my sense of self-worth.

For anyone who has grieved the loss of the fairytale, I want you to know this: You are not alone. This idealized version of life and love was so ingrained in us that we never learned to see ourselves as capable and amazing in our own right. We were taught to wait for someone else to save us. But that was never the truth.

In my experience, I had no sense of self-responsibility. I knew how to be responsible for others—I had been trained to do that—but no one ever taught me to take responsibility for myself. Growing up, I watched how money was always in the hands of men. My parents separated when I was still young, and I saw firsthand how my mother struggled without having been involved in the family finances. My father wasn't particularly good with money either. Some weeks, we had plenty; other weeks, we barely had enough. My mother had no say in how finances were handled, and that dynamic reinforced the idea that money was something men dealt with, leaving me unprepared to manage it myself.

When my marriage ended, it was a moment of awakening for me. I realized that not only had I been grieving the fairytale, but I had also been unconsciously living out patterns of codependency and disempowerment. Many of us were brought up believing that the man was the head of the house and would take care of everything. This belief system created an environment where we were not given the tools to manage our own lives effectively.

For those who feel the grief of the fairy tale, I understand how real that pain is. But I'm here to tell you that once you get to the other side of that grief, there's a new truth waiting for you. You will discover that there were always things you could have done for yourself, decisions you could have made, and boundaries you could have set. You have the power to take responsibility for your own happiness, and you always have.

One of the greatest lessons I've learned is that we must approach relationships consciously. It's not about meeting someone who will save us but about choosing to share our lives with someone while also being responsible for ourselves. This means knowing our values, showing up authentically, and doing the inner work to be the person we want to attract.

Whether your relationship is male/female, female/female, or any other configuration, the principle remains the same: You must show up fully as yourself. You must bring self-responsibility, reliability, trustworthiness, care, and commitment. And you must have done the inner work to understand who you are and what you need in a relationship.

We were never taught these things growing up, but that doesn't mean we can't learn them now. From this moment forward, we get to decide how we show up in our relationships. We get to choose authenticity, we get to do the work, and we get to create something real and meaningful.

So, for anyone out there grieving the loss of their fairy tale, remember this: It was never your fault. It was an illusion we were taught to believe in. Now, you have the power to create a relationship that is real, honest, and fulfilling, not because someone saved you, but because you chose to save yourself.

It won't always be easy. But it will be right.

And it will be worth it.

What was the takeaway from this chapter for you?

....

....

Can you relate to the fairytale and the loss it could have created for you or you have seen this in your experience?

A Turning Point - Tiniroto

The journey to self-discovery and empowerment began with a single book, Feel the Fear and Do It Anyway, by Susan Jeffers. This book was a revelation, a beacon of hope in a life that felt devoid of possibilities. It taught me that fear is a natural part of life, but it doesn't have to control us. We have the power to face our fears, to make choices that align with our true selves, and to create a life that reflects our values and desires.

I wanted my kids to be in a better environment, somewhere where people behaved differently than what was in our neighborhood.

Reading that book marked a pivotal moment in my life. It was the catalyst for a significant decision: to move to Tiniroto with my three children. I wanted a fresh start, away from the chaos and negativity that had defined my life. Tiniroto represented a new chapter, a place where we could build a new life and leave behind the past. However, the transition was not without its challenges.

The Storms of Change

Moving to Tiniroto was a bold step, but it was also fraught with difficulties. The day we moved in, I felt a sense of discovering myself in new ways and relief, believing that things would finally change for the better. But life had other plans. Just three days after our move, I was involved in a car accident. My car was totaled, and I was left without transportation in a remote area. The accident caused a back injury, leading to emergency surgery five months later and a long recovery period.

Tiniroto was an hour from Gisborne, and I rented a house with 20 minutes of gravel, either way, to get back onto the tar-sealed road. The fresh start I sought in the country came with a sense of freedom that was so wonderful to me.

The house I rented was large, with an unfinished tennis court and a magnificent apple tree that yielded more than enough fruit for my family. We had a few animals—a dog named Katie, some rabbits, and a goat we called Sarah.

The open spaces and quiet of the countryside were a stark contrast to the street and neighborhood, where police visited often, and people lived day-to-day in survival mode.

However, despite the change in scenery, I found that many of the same energetic patterns I had known all my life followed me. My thoughts, decisions, and emotions remained much the same.

The fresh start was external; internally I had yet to learn to live from the inside out. The freedom I felt in Tiniroto was primarily physical—free from the expectations and demands of people in the city. But I hadn't yet learned to free my mind and emotions, a lesson that would come much later.

But Tiniroto wasn't just about peace and quiet. It was here that the call came. It was the 4th of July, 1997, a day that should have been one of celebration for my brother Michael. He'd just received the license for a new winery in Cromwell—a dream he'd worked so hard to realize. I could almost picture him, standing proud, ready to take on the world with his partners.

But that dream turned into a nightmare. I still remember the words as they came through the phone, like a punch to the gut. "Michael's gone." The details didn't register at first. Only later did I learn what happened—that he'd gotten some wine from a VAT, and the wine was too low for the tap. Michael was very tall, so he got a jug to get the wine with, and the fumes from the vat had knocked him out, and he never woke up.

I was miles away, trapped by the storm that had closed the roads. I couldn't get to my mother, couldn't be there for her in that moment when she needed me most. I felt helpless, stuck in a place that had once felt like a refuge but now felt like a prison.

The next morning, when the roads cleared, I finally made it into town.

At Michael's funeral, I remember the ache in my heart was matched only by the pain in my body. I was on a walking stick, struggling with the emotional burden and the physical challenge of standing and moving through the day. My father was there, looking more worn than ever, with his divorced wife and his estranged children, well, four of us. There were bits I remember vividly, and other aspects are all blurred into one.

The challenges didn't stop there. There was that unsettling incident with the man on the four-wheeler, who seemed to think he had some kind of claim on me. He'd show up, sitting on the lawn with his rifle. I rang the landlord of the farm, and he banned him from coming up to the house but I didn't feel safe anymore.

It was then that I knew I had to move, so I found a place on the other side of Tiniroto, and it was wonderful, with a tennis court you could play tennis on.

And it started off so well, but when you live in survival mode, plus an outside-in worldview, are triggered by events and people, and lived in a constant turmoil plus anticipation of the next unfortunate event. It was hard enough losing Michael, and then to lose my father just months later in February 1998. He had been a complicated man, and our relationship wasn't always easy, but he was still my father. The grief was different—less sharp, perhaps, but it added another layer to the pain. And then, just 15 months after losing Dad, Mum was gone too. Three deaths in 22 months. My mother didn't recover from losing Michael. Losing a child is extremely difficult. And Michael was our mother's favorite; she had never really gotten over our father, and perhaps the fairytale as well. Too many losses for her, too many years of mental and physical struggle. She had told me just days after my father died that she was going to die; this was several months before the diagnosis of spinal cancer.

Reflection: Tiniroto's Place in My Life

Looking back, Tiniroto was a place of contradictions for me. It was where I found peace and where I faced some of my darkest moments. It was where I learned about resilience, about what it means to keep going, even when life throws the worst at you.

Tiniroto was where I lost my brother and my parents, had a back operation, and spent time on a walking stick, but it was also where I found a strength I didn't know I had. It was a chapter in my life filled with both joy and sorrow. I met some amazing lifelong friends, and though it wasn't easy, it was a part of my story—a part of who I am.

Elements and Finding Joy Beyond Trauma

"Don't allow your past or present condition to control you. It's just a process that you're going through to get you to the next level." —T.D Jakes

Let's have a conversation about something powerful. We all know that life isn't just about reacting to what's happening around us, but often it feels like that's all we do. Sometimes, we become so consumed by our problems, our pain, and our past that it seems like there's no way out. We fall into a habit of reacting, often unconsciously, to the same situations and people. This can trap us in cycles of fear, hurt, or avoidance. When my children were young, I made a decision that changed my life in a way I never expected. My youngest son wanted to play rugby, but there was no coach for his team. So, I stepped up and offered to do it. Little did I know that coaching rugby would become an anchor in my life, giving me structure and purpose at a time when I desperately needed it.

Before I started coaching my life felt chaotic. I lived each day like a leaf blown around in the wind, without any real direction or purpose. I didn't feel good about myself, and life felt as if it was happening to me rather than being something I could actively shape. There was no clear path, no sense of control, and, quite frankly, I was miserable in many ways. But rugby changed that.

I started coaching rugby at Elgin School in Gisborne and later expanded into other sports like softball in the summer. In these activities, I knew what was expected of me; I understood the rules and the boundaries. This gave me a sense of safety and control that was missing in other parts of my life. I thrived in the structure that rugby provided.

Every winter, instead of being stuck at home, I found myself running around on fields, coaching kids. When I moved to Hawkes Bay I got involved on the Hawke's Bay Rugby Union Event team for five years. Rugby was a purposeful and pleasurable activity for me. It wasn't just something I did because I had to—it was something I genuinely enjoyed. I loved rugby, and being involved in it gave me a sense of identity and belonging.

While I don't coach rugby anymore and haven't for quite some time, I still appreciate what it gave me during that period of my life. It was a space where I felt I was playing a meaningful role, and it fit me perfectly. Coaching became more than just a hobby; it was a lifeline. Every other area of my life felt broken, but rugby gave me stability, a sense of purpose, and a way to feel good about myself.

I share this story because many of us may find similar things in our lives—tasks, projects, or hobbies that make us feel purposeful and capable. Maybe you're great at work projects or excel at a particular task, and that brings you a sense of accomplishment and safety. In those moments, we know the boundaries, the expectations, and the outcomes. There's comfort in that certainty.

For some, these activities can become the only area in life where they feel a sense of power and control, especially if other parts of life feel out of control. I experienced this myself—coaching gave me a feeling of authority, but I was conscious of using that power responsibly. Unfortunately, for some, the power they find in these pockets of life can become intoxicating and misused. It's important to be aware of how we handle the power we have, whether it's in work, hobbies, or any other area.

I want to highlight that purposeful and pleasurable activities like these can offer us not only a sense of power but also a chance to impact others positively. When we have structure in one part of our life, it can give us the strength to start unpacking the uncomfortable feelings and unresolved areas in other parts.

As we begin to heal and grow, we can bring that sense of purpose and joy to more areas of our lives, transforming them. Life doesn't have to feel chaotic or out of our control. And as we open up to different perspectives—hearing others' stories and viewpoints—we gain more self-knowledge, which allows us to become even more of who we're meant to be.

But here's something I want you to know — we are not our trauma

What you've been through is part of your story, yes, but it's not the whole story. Your trauma doesn't define you, and it certainly doesn't dictate the rest of your life. Once we move past being reactionary, once we stop focusing so heavily on our pain and start looking for solutions, we open ourselves up to a whole new world of possibilities. In that space, healing begins.

When we stop looking at the problems all the time and start shifting our attention to the solutions, something incredible happens. We begin to realize that we have a choice. Every day we can choose how we respond, how we think, and how we show up in the world. And that's when we start having a different kind of conversation with ourselves—one about who we truly are and what lights us up inside. That's where the concept of elements comes in.

Understanding Your Elements

Let me explain what I mean by "elements." You may have heard the phrase, "Follow your joy." That's a good starting point. Your elements are the things you naturally gravitate towards—the activities, moments, or experiences that give you an immense amount of joy. These are the things that when you're doing them, time seems to disappear. You're not thinking about the outcome or whether you're being productive. You're simply in a state of flow.

I want you to really reflect on that for a moment. Think about the times when you've been so absorbed in something that hours flew by, and when you finally stopped, you felt refreshed, alive, and connected to yourself in a way that words can barely describe. That's your element at work. It's not something you have to do—it's something you're called to do because it nourishes your soul.

"Your element is the place where the things you love and the things you're good at come together." — Ken Robinson

We Are Capable of Many Things, But Not Everything Is Right for Us

Here's where a key realization comes in, just because you can do something doesn't mean it's the right thing for you. That's a game-changer, isn't it? When you realize that you don't have to say yes to every opportunity or fulfill every expectation, you suddenly gain the freedom to make choices that serve you.

This awareness gives you space to align your actions with your true self, to activate the things that make you feel good, not just competent. In doing so, you'll find a connection to yourself, your purpose, and the world around you.

Let me share some examples of my elements. For me, one of my elements is drawing or painting. When I sit down with my art, time just disappears. I get so engrossed in what I'm doing that I forget about the clock, the to-do lists, and the outside world. I'm in my own world, and I love it. When I finish, I feel lighter, happier, and more relaxed.

Another one of my elements is reading. I could spend hours curled up with a good book, and when I do, I feel like I've traveled somewhere new and experienced something deeper, even if I haven't left my home. Reading is an escape, but it's also a journey into new thoughts and ideas and that brings me joy.

Joy Comes From Within

Joy, true joy, doesn't come from external sources. It's an inside job. It radiates out into our lives from within us. That's what makes elements so important—they connect us to that inner joy. When we focus on these elements, we're not just passing the time; we're engaging in something that fills us up from the inside out.

So, now it's time to explore your elements.

Discovering Your Elements

I want you to take a moment to reflect on what your elements might be. These are things you naturally enjoy, things that make you feel more alive, energized, and content. What are those activities for you? Maybe it's cooking, gardening, or exercising. Maybe it's singing, dancing, or writing. The point is to find things that make you feel good—not because someone else said they're good for you, but because they feel good to you.

Take a moment, grab a pen, and write down 5 to 10 things you think might be your elements. Ready?

From Elements to Hobbies

Now that you have your list of elements let's take this a step further. Is there anything on that list that you could turn into a hobby? By that, I mean something you do regularly, simply for the joy of it. A hobby doesn't have to be productive or have a specific goal. It's something you do because it brings you pleasure and purpose. It recharges you mentally, emotionally, and even physically.

Look at your list. What could you turn into a regular hobby? Maybe it's gardening, or perhaps it's writing poetry, cooking new dishes, or learning to play an instrument. Hobbies are one of the most undervalued parts of life. We often don't give them the credit they deserve. But hobbies are powerful because they feed your soul in a way that your day-to-day tasks and responsibilities often can't.

Here's another list for you to fill in. Write down 1 to 5 things from your element list that you could turn into a hobby.

A Commitment to Yourself

Now that you've reflected on your elements and considered turning them into hobbies, it's time to make a commitment. One of the best things you can do for your mental, emotional, and physical well-being is to regularly engage in these activities. When you do things that bring you joy and connect you to your inner self you're recharging your spirit. And when your spirit is full, you can give more to the people and things around you.

I want you to make this commitment to yourself:

I commit to finding a regular hobby within the next three months that feeds my soul and brings me joy. I agree that this will be my time to connect with myself, and I will incorporate it into my life.

Take a deep breath and let that settle in. You deserve this time. You deserve joy. You deserve to be connected to yourself, not just through the lens of trauma or past experiences, but through the things that light you up and make you feel truly alive.

Love Languages and the Power of Choice

Before we finish, let's talk about love languages for a moment. Just as we have elements that connect us to ourselves, we also have love languages that connect us to others. Understanding how we give and receive love can be transformative, especially when we're no longer living in a reactive space. When we understand our love language—whether it's words of affirmation, acts of service, quality time, physical touch, or receiving gifts— we can communicate more effectively and build stronger relationships.

But here's the key: Just like with elements, your love language is personal. It's not dictated by anyone else's expectations. It's about how you naturally connect, feel fulfilled, and show affection.

Moving Forward

As you continue your journey, remember that you are not your trauma. You are capable of making choices that nourish your soul, and by understanding your elements and love languages, you can create a life filled with more joy, more connection, and more purpose. Keep reflecting, keep exploring, and most importantly, keep choosing yourself.

This chapter has been a conversation, but now it's your turn to take action.

Write down your reflections, commit to discovering and nurturing your elements, and make time for the things that bring you joy. The solutions you're looking for.

They're already within you, just waiting to be uncovered. Write down up to 10 things that when you do them, it feels like flow, and it feels easy.

I invite you to reconnect with the elements of your life that feel easy, natural, and joyful. These are the things that light you up from the inside out—the passions, hobbies, and instincts that draw you in effortlessly. As children, these elements came naturally to us, sparking curiosity and joy, but too often, they were diminished or dismissed by others or even by ourselves.

Why? Because we've been conditioned to believe that ease is unearned, that struggle is required to be worthy of success. Society tells us: if we haven't struggled, if we haven't faced hardship, then we haven't earned the right to enjoy what we achieve. But here's the truth: when we embrace struggle as a constant, we forget how to recognize satisfaction. We stop appreciating the beauty of flow, where things come together in harmony.

You see, we all have elements—those natural, personal inclinations that bring us joy, fulfillment, and a sense of purpose. And when we follow them, we enter a state of flow where life seems to work for us rather than against us. In this space, we can give effort without feeling the weight of struggle. The effort is there, but it's joyful, aligned with who we truly are and what matters to us.

Whether it's cooking, dancing, painting, or even something like organizing or storytelling, when you're in your element, you feel good. And when you feel good, you are living from the inside out. That's the key to real satisfaction and growth.

But many of us have been taught to overlook these elements, to prioritize struggle and hard work because we've been told that's what it takes to succeed. So instead of pursuing what comes naturally to us, we take on things that belong to others—things that worked for someone else but don't necessarily resonate with us. We squeeze ourselves into molds that were never meant for us, thinking that maybe if we struggle hard enough, we'll find success or happiness. But all the while, we're ignoring the very things that would bring us real joy.

So, I challenge you to reflect back to when you were a child. What drew you in? What made you feel alive? Were you a storyteller? An artist? A dancer? These elements are your guiding lights, and they're still within you, waiting to be rediscovered. When you follow them, you'll find that life doesn't need to be a constant struggle. You'll experience flow, purpose, and a deep sense of satisfaction.

Now, I encourage you to take action: write down ten of your elements. What comes easily to you? What feels natural? And once you've identified them, make a commitment to yourself—act on one of these elements in the next ten days.

When we start living in alignment with our elements, life changes from the inside out. The satisfaction, joy, and purpose that we've been chasing out there, we realize, was always inside us.

The Illusion of Powerlessness

Life can often feel like an unpredictable storm, with events crashing down like wave's, leaving us feeling overwhelmed and helpless. In those moments, it's easy to believe that we have no control over our circumstances and that we are merely victims of fate. This mindset creates a cycle of negativity, where our thoughts and emotions attract more of the same. It's a state of living in constant fear, expecting the worst, and bracing for impact.

The Cycle of Vigilance and Expectation

You wake up each day not anticipating joy or success but dreading the inevitable hardships. It's not that you actively plan for bad things to happen, but rather, you carry an unspoken belief that they will. This belief shapes your reality, creating a self-fulfilling prophecy. The mindset of "life is out to get me" becomes ingrained, and every negative experience serves as evidence to reinforce it. It's a vicious cycle where the expectation of misfortune brings about more misfortune.Living in this state of vigilance is exhausting. You're always on high alert, scanning for threats and preparing for the next crisis. This hyper-awareness is a defense mechanism, a way to protect yourself from further pain.

However, it also perpetuates a life filled with anxiety and stress. The belief that you deserve the hardships you face is a heavy burden, one that keeps you trapped in a loop of negativity and self-doubt.

The Weight of Being "Nice"

In addition to the constant vigilance, there's the pressure to be nice, to fit into societal expectations, and to avoid rocking the boat. For me, this meant becoming a doormat, always putting others' needs before my own. I believed that if I could just be agreeable enough if I could make myself useful, then maybe I would be liked and appreciated. This desire to fit in, to be accepted, led me to sacrifice my own happiness and self-respect.

This pressure to be nice can stem from various sources, such as family dynamics, cultural norms, and societal expectations. We are often conditioned from a young age to prioritize the happiness and comfort of others over our own. We are taught to be polite, to avoid conflict, and to always put others first. While kindness and consideration for others are certainly important qualities, there is a fine line between being genuinely kind and sacrificing our own well-being.

When we constantly strive to be nice, we may find ourselves tiptoeing around difficult conversations or suppressing our own needs and desires. We fear rejection, confrontation, or even being labeled as selfish. We may believe that our worth lies in pleasing others and that failing to do so means we are somehow unworthy or unlovable.

This pressure can be especially tough for individuals who are empathetic and highly attuned to the emotions of others. We may feel the need to take on the emotional burdens of others, to be the peacemaker in every situation, and to rescue and fix people's problems constantly. This is not only exhausting, but it also prevents us from fully living our own lives and pursuing our own goals and passions.

The weight of being nice can also lead to a lack of authenticity. We may feel the need to wear masks to hide our true thoughts and feelings in order to maintain harmony and avoid conflict. We become chameleons, adapting ourselves to fit the expectations and desires of others. In doing so, we dim our own light and lose touch with our true selves.

Breaking free from the weight of being nice requires a deep exploration of our own values, needs, and boundaries. It involves learning to listen to and honor our own inner voice, even if it means disappointing or upsetting others in the process. It means developing the courage to assert our opinions and desires, knowing that our worth is not tied to the approval of others.

It's important to recognize that being kind and considerate does not require sacrificing our own well-being. We can still be compassionate and empathetic while also prioritizing our own needs. This requires learning to set and communicate clear boundaries, saying no when necessary, and surrounding ourselves with people who respect and appreciate us for who we truly are.

Shedding the weight of being nice takes time and practice. It may involve unlearning deeply ingrained patterns of behavior and challenging long-held beliefs about our own worth and the nature of relationships. But by doing so, we can reclaim our authenticity, cultivate healthier relationships, and experience a greater sense of self-worth and fulfillment. It's a journey toward self-acceptance and self-compassion, where we honor and prioritize our own needs as much as we do those of others.

I found myself in relationships where I was needed but not valued. I became the caretaker, the one who cooked, cleaned, and accommodated others' needs. This dynamic played out in various areas of my life, from friendships to romantic relationships. I believed that being needed equated to being loved, but in reality, it left me feeling used and unappreciated. It took a long time for me to realize that my worth was not tied to what I could do for others. I deserved to be loved for who I was, not for what I could provide.

The Fairy Elephant Effect

Years after J.M. struggled through her own childhood, her mother read her a letter that had been written by J.M.'s grandfather to his wife about his own children. In the letter, he called J.M.'s mother "dumb" in certain areas of her life. The irony wasn't lost on J.M. Her mother, who had unintentionally passed on her feelings of inadequacy, had herself been labeled and burdened with similar beliefs.

J.M.'s mother went on to defy those expectations by earning a degree in physiotherapy, breaking the cycle in her own way. This revelation hit J.M. hard. She saw how easily other people's frustrations, fears, and limitations could be projected onto a small child and how those words could shape entire lives.

Understanding this generational pain gave J.M. the strength to stop the cycle. She began to rewrite her story, no longer believing the labels placed on her by others. J.M. realized that while she had been born into a history of struggle and low self-worth, she had the power to rise above it, just as her mother had. She wasn't "dumb," nor was she defined by her dyslexia or the anger from her childhood. She was strong, capable, and worthy of love and success.

J. M.

Interrupting Overthinking and Worrying Techniques

5-4-3-2-1 Grounding Technique

This is a simple mindfulness exercise that brings your focus back to the present moment, breaking the cycle of overthinking.

Acknowledge 5 things you can see around you.

Acknowledge 4 things you can touch.

Acknowledge 3 things you can hear.

Acknowledge 2 things you can smell.

Acknowledge 1 thing you can taste.

Example: If you're spiraling into worry about a future event, use this exercise to ground yourself and reset your thoughts.

Cups

"The loveliest thing you can do for yourself is to embrace the beauty of your humanness" —Susan Jeffers

And so we continue. Let's take a deep breath here because I want you to really feel this: you are enough. That's right—right here, right now, as you are. You don't need to do, do do, or achieve a monumental list of things to prove your worth. You are worthy just by being YOU.

Let that sink in. You don't have to hustle yourself into exhaustion just to feel a sense of validation. We need to stop the doing and start the BEING.

When we focus too much on doing—on ticking off tasks from our never-ending list—we lose sight of who we really are. We become disconnected from our own inner voice. And that voice? It's there, patiently waiting for you to listen, to respond rather than react to life. It's like driving a car full of fear, anxiety, and overwhelm, frantically trying to control everything. But what happens when we switch lanes? What happens when we turn onto that road of trust, ease, and self-compassion?

Magic. That's what happens. And it's not the magic of fairy tales—no, this is the real magic of life aligning with who you truly are. When you stop overthinking, when you let go of the need to know and control everything, you allow space for new opportunities to flow in. Inspired action follows when we trust.

Because here's the truth: overthinking, anxiousness, and overwhelm—they're signs that we don't feel safe within ourselves. And when we don't feel safe, we cling to control. We get caught up in worst-case scenarios and catastrophizing, imagining all the things that could go wrong, and before we know it, we've already emotionally lived through a disaster that hasn't even happened. Stop. We need to stop living in future fears and start living in present possibilities.

This is not just about turning off that highway of fear and doubt. It's about packing your car differently, my friend. Right now, your car might be packed with heavy, unnecessary baggage—worry, guilt, shame, self-criticism. But what if you repack? What if you filled your life with joy, purpose, and pleasure instead? What if you put on your "big girl boots" (or "big boy boots") and filled yourself with courage, commitment, and consistency?

You'd feel unstoppable, right? You'd start to see that small, actionable, purposeful steps taken daily add up to a life you truly love. Consistency is key, and it's not about perfection. It's about progress. Each step forward, no matter how small, is building momentum. You don't need to achieve everything in 24 hours—Rome wasn't built in a day, and neither is the life you desire. But brick by brick, action by action, you are building something beautiful.

"You matter simply because you exist. Your worth is not tied to what you've done or haven't done." —Anonymous

Now, let's talk about the list. Because we all have that list—whether we've written it down or not. And for many of us, that list is filled with things we think we need to do to be worthy of love, success, or even our own approval. But guess what? That list? It's nonsense. Throw it away. Instead, make a new list, a meaningful list. A list that serves you.

On this new list, you'll find things like:

Meditation

Breathing exercises

Power statements or affirmations

Journaling or Morning Pages

Daily movement or exercise

Learning a new skill

Cultivating hobbies

Nurturing relationships

Practicing spirituality in whatever form resonates with you

These are the things that, when done daily, weekly, and monthly, will accumulate into a life that you lead. Because remember that : you are in the driver's seat. You are the power. The only difference is which direction you're facing, and today, I invite you to face the direction of your dreams.

When we start filling our cup with new thoughts, new feelings, and new actions, something amazing happens. The old stuff—the guilt, the shame, the unworthiness—starts to float to the surface. And as it rises, we can thank it for the role it played and then let it go. With each new day, as you fill your life with more joy and purpose, those negative emotions start to dissolve. They lose their grip on you.

Suddenly, you'll find yourself looking out at a whole new horizon. You'll start to see yourself as the magnificent person you've always been—the person you like, the person you love. You'll look in the mirror and say, "I like you. I'm proud of you. You've done the work, and you're reaping the rewards."

And you'll realize something so incredibly freeing: life supports you. More good can come into your life every day, and the best part? You're the one creating it. You're the one taking those inspired, aligned actions. You're the one shifting your energy from fear to love, from doubt to confidence, from "not enough" to more than enough.

So let's keep going. Let's keep repeating this because sometimes we need to hear it more than once: You are enough. You are powerful. You are capable. Every day, you're getting closer to the life you desire, not by doing more but by being more of who you are. You've got this.

My Cup Overflows with Clarity

When we focus solely on the problem, we trap ourselves in a cycle that reinforces the very thing we're trying to escape. It's like swimming in quicksand, the more we struggle, the deeper we sink. And so often, we become so accustomed to the weight of the problem, the heaviness of it, that we don't even realize how much space it's taking up in our lives. We focus on what's wrong, replay the same stories in our heads, and remain in that emotional loop, completely disconnected from the present.

This mindset doesn't help us live in the here and now; it keeps us anchored to the past and fearful of the future. When all we see is the problem, the problem becomes all there is. But we have to remember—we are not our problems. We are far more than the patterns and emotional imprints that shaped us. We are creators, and the moment we start introducing new ways of thinking, feeling, and acting, our cup begins to overflow with clarity and possibility.

It's a process. Just like EFT (Emotional Freedom Techniques) which you will learn about The EFT chapter , it teaches us to release old emotional energy, we also need to replace that space with something new. Our cup doesn't stay empty for long—it's either filled with old habits and limiting beliefs, or we intentionally fill it with thoughts and actions that uplift us. When we take that conscious step to repack our vessel with fresh energy, we open ourselves up to a deeper transformation. Slowly, the old "us," the one who was weighed down by pain and negative narratives, begins to spill over the edge and fall away. And it happens more easily and safely than we might expect because we are making space for something more meaningful, more aligned with the person we truly want to be.

This process creates a much-needed emotional breath. It's as if we've been holding on to all this tension, all these unresolved feelings, and for the first time in a long time, we can finally exhale. There's a lightness in that release. A space that opens up where the old weight used to be. And that breath—it's not just physical; it's emotional, mental, and spiritual. It's like seeing the world with new eyes. We begin to notice the things that have always been there but were hidden under the fog of our old emotional state.

Our cup doesn't just empty; it overflows with clarity, fresh energy, and with new perspectives. It's not just that we've released what was no longer serving us—it's that we've replaced it with thoughts, emotions, and actions that elevate us. We begin to see the world differently because we are different. Our inner state shifts, and as a result, the way we interact with life changes too.

This is where the real magic happens. When you start shifting your focus away from the problem, and toward the life you want to create, you are no longer just reacting to life—you're responding with intention. You become the architect of your own experience. The old, familiar patterns that once felt so ingrained start to feel foreign. The stories that used to define you begin to lose their grip. You stop identifying with the problem and start connecting with the solution.

It's a delicate balance—unpacking the old while simultaneously repacking the new. It's not enough to just take things out; we must also introduce what will help us move forward. We must anchor ourselves to the present while casting a vision for the future. And here's the truth: it doesn't matter if you only manage to shift for five minutes a day. Those five minutes matter. Each small step you take toward a new way of being interrupts the old pattern, and with consistency, those interruptions become the new norm.

The more we do this, the more the unfamiliar becomes familiar. The more the new "us" starts to feel like the real "us." And before we know it, our entire way of being has shifted. We're no longer navigating life from the perspective of the old stories and emotions that used to rule us. We've created something new—a life that is aligned with who we truly are, a life that feels purposeful, empowered, and free.

When our cup overflows with clarity, it's not that life stops challenging us. It's that we are now able to respond to those challenges from a place of strength, awareness, and peace. We've done the work. We've unpacked the old and introduced the new. We've created a life where our emotional state no longer controls us—we control it.

And that's the beauty of this journey. As we release the old and embrace the new, not only do we transform ourselves, but we also transform the lives of those around us. The energy we put into the world shifts, and the people in our orbit feel that change. We are no longer just surviving; we are thriving. We are creating lives filled with meaning, purpose, and pleasure. And that is when our cup truly overflows.

In this chapter, you'll see the paintings I've done of the five cups, each representing a stage of the journey toward meaningful change. These illustrations reflect the process we all go through as we begin to reshape our lives, moving from chaos and self-doubt toward clarity and self-compassion. Each cup symbolizes a pivotal stage, a marker of where you are and what's unfolding within you. Recognize where you stand on this path, and know that every step forward, no matter how small, brings you closer to creating the life you deserve. Keep filling your cup with what serves you. Keep unpacking and repacking your beliefs and experiences. Soon, your life will overflow with all that is good, clear, and true.

As an outcome coach, I believe that we become what we believe we are. I focus on purposeful and pleasurable goals, guiding clients to connect with who they want to be, what they want to have, and how they want to feel. These aren't just targets to reach; they are a way of being in the present, evolving into more as we take meaningful steps toward our vision.

I believe in balancing the present with the past. If we stay stuck in our past stories, we can never ground ourselves in the present or activate the skills and characteristics we need to thrive today. Life is about more than just healing; it's about finding joy and satisfaction from the inside out and understanding that progress—no matter how small—matters.

In our work together, I use a variety of tools, including EFT tapping, to help clients release blocks and align their energy with their desired outcomes. We set both Ends goals—feeling and seeing the future self they want to become—and Means goals, which are the actionable steps to achieve that vision. This process isn't just about hitting milestones; it's about embracing a joyful, purposeful journey that aligns with their true essence.

By combining EFT tapping with other tools and techniques, I help clients clear limiting beliefs, stay consistent, and cultivate discipline and self-determination. Together, we create a mindset that allows them to live powerfully in the present while continuously growing toward their greater goals, making the journey itself as rewarding as the destination.

I aim to help you find grounding, to remind you that who you are right now is enough and that you can create emotional and mental breathing space while unpacking those overwhelming and intense responses to past events. Life doesn't have to be about reliving our pain forever. Instead, we make space to grow and evolve, all while knowing we are okay in the present moment.

Cup 1:
Awareness of the Negative Story

As you look at the first cup, recognize how many of us have been in this place. I certainly have. This cup represents the swirling chaos in our lives. At times, it may seem calm, but more often, it feels like an eruption. In this stage, I was hyper-vigilant, constantly scanning for the next catastrophe. Hypervigilance isn't about being weak or unworthy; it's a survival mechanism. Survivors stand up not because they want to but because they have to. It's how we keep moving forward when it feels like the world is collapsing around us.

This first cup holds some good, but it's overshadowed by the negative. Every one of us has some good happening in our lives, but the bad often takes over our focus. We tell ourselves stories like "I'm not enough," "It's all my fault," "I can't get it right," or "Life is out to get me." These thoughts weave emotional threads in our bodies, and the more threads we gather, the more tangled and overwhelming they become. This mental chaos fills our cup, swirling endlessly, and we're left feeling powerless and lost in our own minds.

"The first step toward change is awareness. The second step is acceptance." – Nathaniel Branden

Negative Story/Narrative:

"I am not good enough. Everything I do turns out wrong. Life is against me."

"I am a burden, and I don't deserve happiness or success."

Emotional/Mental States:

Overwhelmed, fearful, anxious, self-critical, unworthy, defeated

The constant inner dialogue of negativity and self-doubt

How We May Show Up in Life:

Over-anxious, hypervigilant, self-sabotaging

Avoids risks, struggles to trust others, defensive or overly withdrawn

Exhausted from trying to please everyone or avoid failure

New Thoughts and Beliefs to Add to the Cup:

"I am enough, just as I am."

"I am worthy of love and success."

"I deserve good things, and I am learning to trust myself."

"My mistakes do not define me; they help me grow."

"I am a work in progress, and that's okay."

Cup 2:
Facing Emotional Reactions and Mental Chaos

In the second cup, a shift begins to happen. You might have decided to make a different choice, started working with someone, or begun consuming new information. A bit of good starts flowing in, but with it comes the old negative stuff from the bottom of the cup. As new ideas and experiences emerge, the negative patterns bubble up, but now you see them differently. You recognize the thoughts, the emotions, the patterns.

Here's where the choice arises: You can either let the negativity define you and fall back into old habits, or you can acknowledge it as a part of you that's surfacing for healing. Instead of being stuck, you start to see these patterns for what they are—outdated beliefs about yourself. And on the other side of this awareness new thoughts begin to form: "I am enough," "I am not broken," "Good things can happen to me," "I am worthy of love and success."

Even if these new beliefs don't feel entirely real at first, you've started something. The old patterns may spill over the edge of the cup, but with each new thought you're allowing more space for positivity and self-compassion to take root.

Negative Story/Narrative:

"I have to be perfect to be accepted. If I don't control everything, things will fall apart."

"If I let people see the real me, they won't like me."

Emotional/Mental States:

Fear of judgment, perfectionism, guilt, shame, over-control

Constantly thinking about the worst-case scenario, feeling out of control.

How We May Show Up in Life:

Hyper-vigilant, micromanaging, controlling, perfectionist

Avoids vulnerability, keeps emotions bottled up, people-pleasing

Easily frustrated when things don't go as planned, burned out.

New Thoughts and Beliefs to Add to the Cup:

"I can let go of control and trust that I am safe."

"Perfection is not required for love and acceptance."

"It's okay to be vulnerable; I am still strong."

"I don't have to do everything myself. It's safe to ask for help."

"I release the need to control and allow life to unfold naturally."

"You are allowed to be both a masterpiece and a work in progress simultaneously." – Sophia Bush

Cup 3:
Overcoming Numbness and Anger

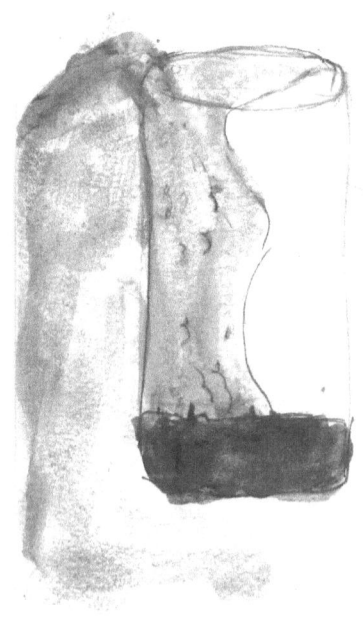

In the third cup, the process deepens. As you allow new beliefs in, you may find yourself more aware of when and how you fall back into negativity. It's not about erasing all of your past experiences but about learning to shift your response to them. You begin to notice when you react out of fear or self-doubt, and in those moments, you pause. You start to question the old narrative: "Is this really true? Does this story serve me anymore?" With this awareness comes more freedom, as you choose to let go of what no longer serves you.

In this stage, you're still in the midst of change, but the self-critical voice begins to lose its grip. Instead of berating yourself for past mistakes or feeling unworthy, you start to speak to yourself with kindness and understanding. You're slowly reprogramming your mind to believe that you are enough, that you deserve good things, and that life is working in your favor.

In this stage, individuals are beginning to confront long-buried emotions, such as numbness and anger that have been ignored or suppressed for a long time. This is part of what you refer to as "cup three." By reaching this stage, the individual has already activated the previous "cups" or layers of emotional processing, which have likely helped build inner safety, stability, and resilience. These foundations now allow the person to finally face and process the more uncomfortable and challenging emotions.

Numbness often serves as a defense mechanism, a way of blocking out overwhelming feelings that might have seemed too dangerous or painful to confront in the past. It's a kind of emotional shutdown where the individual becomes disconnected from their feelings to survive difficult experiences. Anger, on the other hand, might also act as a shield, often protecting the person from vulnerability. Anger is commonly a secondary emotion, masking more vulnerable feelings like hurt, sadness, or fear.

The earlier steps in emotional healing—the activation of previous "cups"—have laid a groundwork of self-awareness, self-compassion, and emotional regulation. This creates an environment where the individual feels safer to confront the repressed emotions. Before, acknowledging these emotions may have seemed too overwhelming or dangerous. Now, with that sense of internal safety in place, there is less fear of being swallowed by the intensity of those feelings.

In this stage it's important to recognize that numbness and anger had their purpose. They were mechanisms that protected the person during periods of vulnerability or trauma. Instead of rejecting or shaming oneself for having suppressed these emotions, they can be acknowledged for their role in emotional survival. This act of acknowledgment helps to break the cycle of suppression, offering a form of release.

Letting Go

Once these emotions are acknowledged and understood, they can be processed and ultimately released. Letting go doesn't mean forgetting the past or pretending it didn't hurt. Instead, it means releasing the emotional hold these feelings had over the person's present life. By allowing space for them to be fully felt and understood, the individual can integrate the experience and move forward without the weight of repressed anger or numbness.

This stage is empowering, as it allows the individual to reclaim their emotional freedom. After all, the energy that once went into avoiding or suppressing these feelings can now be directed toward healing, growth, and more authentic living.

Negative Story/Narrative:

"It's safer to shut down than to feel. If I let myself feel, I'll be overwhelmed."

"Everyone leaves, and no one really cares about me."

Emotional/Mental States:

Numb, disconnected, lonely, resentful, angry, bitter

Cycles of shutting down and feeling emotionally distant, followed by bursts of anger or irritability

How We May Show Up in Life:

Numb, distant, emotionally unavailable, pushing people away

Avoiding deep relationships, lashing out in frustration, isolating oneself

Struggling with vulnerability, difficulty expressing emotions, easily angered by perceived rejection

New Thoughts and Beliefs to Add to the Cup:

"I am allowed to feel and express my emotions safely."

"I deserve to be supported and understood."

"It's safe to let others in; I don't have to do this alone."

"My anger is a signal for deeper feelings that I am willing to explore."

"I am open to receiving love and connection."

***"Success is the sum of small efforts, repeated day in and day out."* – Robert Collier**

Cup 4:
Releasing Guilt and Self-Blame

By the time you reach the fourth cup, you're in a place of greater peace. You've made progress in rewriting your narrative, and though challenges still arise, they don't knock you off balance as easily as they once did. You're more aware of your emotional responses, and you've learned to manage them with greater ease.

You've filled your cup with thoughts of worthiness, self-love, and acceptance, and while the old patterns still try to creep in, they don't hold the same power. You've started to believe, in both your mind and heart, that you deserve the good things life has to offer.

Negative Story/Narrative:

"It's all my fault. If I had been better, things wouldn't have gone wrong."

"I have to fix everything for everyone."

Emotional/Mental States:

Guilt, shame, self-blame, over-responsibility, resentment

Constantly replaying past mistakes, obsessing over what could have been done differently

How We May Show Up in Life:

Being over-apologetic takes on too much responsibility, can't say no

Resentful of others, especially when they don't appreciate sacrifices

Overburdened by guilt, emotionally drained from carrying others' weight

New Thoughts and Beliefs to Add to the Cup:

"I am not responsible for everyone's happiness."

"I forgive myself for my past mistakes and move forward with compassion."

"I release the need to blame myself for things beyond my control."

"I am allowed to prioritize my own needs without guilt."

"I am enough and I don't have to prove my worth through overdoing."

"It's believing in our dreams and facing our fears head-on that allows us to live our lives beyond limits." — Amy Purdy

Cup 5: Tipping Point and Clarity

This cup gives us the opportunity to finally have inner trust. The secret ingredient to living freely and fully.

No light
living + Releasing of youngs

Finally, the fifth cup represents clarity and wholeness. You've done the work of unpacking the negative stories, and now your cup is filled with new, empowering beliefs. You feel grounded in who you are, no longer defined by your past or by the narratives that once controlled you.

At this stage, your life begins to overflow with all that is good, clear, and true. You've embraced the idea that growth is a journey, not a destination, and you continue to move forward, step by step, knowing that you are worthy, capable, and deserving of a life filled with joy, peace, and purpose.

Negative Story/Narrative

"I can't trust myself to make good decisions. I'll always fail."

"It's too late for me to change my life."

Emotional/Mental States:

Fear of failure, indecision, lack of confidence, hopelessness, exhaustion

Stuck in analysis paralysis, fear of taking action due to potential failure

How We May have Shown Up in Life:

Procrastination, avoiding responsibility, second-guessing every decision

Stuck in the same cycles, feeling powerless to change circumstances

Allowing fear to dictate choices, resisting growth, afraid to commit

New Thoughts and Beliefs to Add to the Cup:

"I trust myself to make decisions that are aligned with my highest good."

"It's never too late to create the life I want."

"I am capable of change, and I deserve the best version of life."

"I embrace the unknown with courage and confidence."

"I release the fear of failure and choose to move forward with clarity."

Summary of New Thoughts and Beliefs for Each Cup

Cup 1: Recognize your worth and begin to shift your self-perception.

Cup 2: Let go of control and perfectionism, allowing space for vulnerability.

Cup 3: Open up emotionally and embrace deeper connections with yourself and others.

Cup 4: Release guilt and over-responsibility, forgiving yourself and setting healthy boundaries.

Step into clarity, trust your ability to make decisions, and move forward confidently.

The journey from negative self-talk and limiting beliefs to a mindset rooted in self-trust, courage, and confidence is transformative but not always linear. While adopting new empowering beliefs is a powerful step, it's important to recognize the potential setbacks and challenges that can arise along the way. Understanding these will help maintain progress and avoid slipping back into old patterns.

These beliefs offer a more empowered perspective. You're now trusting yourself more, viewing life as filled with potential, and seeing challenges as opportunities rather than obstacles. However, the road forward isn't always smooth. There are common hiccups that can cause you to revert back to old habits if you're not mindful.

Even though the new beliefs feel empowering, when faced with a challenging decision, you might revert to indecision or procrastination because those behaviors feel safer. The brain craves predictability, and change—even positive change—can feel uncomfortable.

You may find yourself second-guessing your choices again or fearing that you'll fail, which brings back the old narratives of "I can't trust myself" or "I'm not capable."

Without being consistent, the old limiting beliefs may resurface because the internal work hasn't fully solidified. For example, you may stop reinforcing positive self-talk or avoid taking courageous actions, slipping back into fear of failure or procrastination.

To stay in the flow of these new, positive beliefs, you need continuous nurturing and self-awareness.

Setbacks will inevitably occur. The key is not to let a slip become a spiral. When you notice yourself reverting to old patterns, practice self-compassion rather than harsh judgment. Acknowledge that progress isn't linear and that each step back is an opportunity to learn and reinforce your growth.

Achieving lasting change requires ongoing attention and consistent action. Slipping back into old patterns is a natural part of the process, but with awareness and tools, you can recover more quickly and continue to move forward. Recognizing these potential hiccups and maintaining a mindset of curiosity and compassion toward yourself will keep you on track toward the life you're creating.

By staying present, acknowledging when you're veering off course, and regularly engaging in practices that reinforce your new beliefs, you'll remain forward-moving and confident in your ability to create the life you want.

"The hardest part of the journey is taking the first step. But once you move, momentum builds. Keep moving." — Author Unknown

"You matter because you are here. Your journey is meaningful, and your worth is infinite." — Elysabeth Wolter

"You are not responsible for fixing everything that is broken. You are responsible for choosing to love yourself enough to be whole." Unknown

"The language used in telling our personal story affects us. We reflect our mind chatter." — Kilroy J. Oldster, Dead Toad Scrolls

Breaking Free from the Past

Stop Nursing, Cursing, and Rehearsing

As Tim Storey wisely put it, "Nurse it, curse it, and rehearse it" only keeps us anchored to the past.

To move forward, we must starve our doubts, believe in the possibility of change, and pause to acknowledge our progress.

This journey towards healing requires a conscious decision to shift our focus from the needs and expectations of others to our own aspirations. By making this choice, we can begin to rebuild our sense of self, reclaim our power, and chart a new course toward a life defined by our own values, aspirations, and dreams.

It's time to stop nursing, cursing, and rehearsing the old stories that hold us back. We all have moments when we felt comforted by the attention our sad stories brought us, but those stories never truly lifted us out of the holes we kept digging. They were like old letters from past situations or people replayed repeatedly in our minds. It's so easy to reach for those stories and the familiar emotions they bring. But there comes a time when we must move on, burn the letters, and write a new chapter.

Right now, you can make a decision to let go of the past. Grab a piece of paper and reflect on the areas where you're still holding on. Acknowledge that for a long time, you may not have known how to help yourself. You might have been the person everyone turned to with their problems, often seeing sides of people that others in your circle never saw. This can blur the lines between where you end and others begin, creating confusion and emotional turmoil.

The Inside Job

Living a fulfilled life is an inside job. It requires due diligence on our thoughts, beliefs, and actions. If you're still blaming others for your problems, you're not taking full responsibility for your life. As a wise person once said, if you're still talking about past grievances, you're nursing, cursing, and rehearsing them. To move forward, you need to let go of these old stories and make new decisions.

Take, for example, a participant in my Release and Re-align program. When she first attended one of my workshops, she felt burdened by old patterns and stories. Through our work together, she was able to release these burdens and feel empowered. She now makes different decisions and no longer picks up the emotional baggage that used to weigh her down. This transformation is possible for anyone willing to do the work.

Embracing New Habits

To create lasting change, we must develop new habits. At first, these habits may feel uncomfortable or out of place, but over time, they become a natural part of who we are. For me, habits like rebounding, morning pages, meditation, and affirmations have become essential. They've always been a part of me, waiting for the emotional disruptions to clear away. Now, they are integral to my daily life, helping me choose my thoughts, actions, and overall outlook.

The Power of Choice

Every human being has the power of choice. This gift allows us to shape our lives and break free from the cycles of the past. If your life feels stagnant or unfulfilling, you have the power to choose a different path. It's not about the destination; it's about the progress you make along the way. Even small steps toward change can lead to significant transformations.

Moving Beyond the Past

Letting go of the past isn't easy, but it's essential. One of the most effective tools I've found for this is EFT tapping. It allows us to release emotional ties and make space for new, positive experiences. Whether you choose to work with me one-on-one or explore the techniques on your own, the goal is to become the magic in your own life.

Removing Limiting Language

Words have power. Phrases like "wish" and "desire" often imply a lack of control or uncertainty. Instead, use words that reflect your intentions and capabilities. Speak of inspiration, creation, and purpose. You have the power to create a life that pulls you forward, filled with meaningful progress and fulfillment.

A New Beginning

I know that starting this journey can feel overwhelming, especially if you're already exhausted from living in negative, draining patterns. But I promise you, the work is worth it. It's the most rewarding work you can do, and the results will transform your life. Start small, focus on one new habit, and watch as your energy and focus shift toward the life you truly want to live.

Remember, you have the power to choose. Your past does not define you, and you can create a new story filled with purpose, joy, and fulfillment. Let go of the old narratives and embrace the possibilities of a brighter future

The script of our lives is often authored by our beliefs, values, and the stories we've accumulated over time. If these beliefs and narratives no longer serve us, we possess the power to rewrite the narrative. Often though we keep recycling them and hoping and or wishing for a new outcome.

Those words and actions are mere reflections of our inner world, and by transforming our thoughts, we can craft a new story for ourselves.

This transformation can be achieved through various techniques like challenging limiting beliefs, practicing positive affirmations, visualization, EFT tapping, mindfulness and more.

Over time, these efforts can lead to a greater sense of contentment, inner peace, and reduced stress, creating a more fulfilling and satisfying life.

Once you realize that you get to make new choices, you will want to start to use your words more intentionally.

As it is our internal and external Language, that shapes our lives.

That is where you have the greatest influence in life. If you are sad, it often comes from your heart and affects your language, and it also can affect your body. How we stand, sit, walk and talk is all affected by our thoughts. Which are words made into sentences. Illnesses can appear out of nowhere, some of these are a direct result of what we think and the script we run in the background day after day. It is often hidden from view, because of limiting beliefs, trauma, environment, sickness, disease, and work-family life balance.

When you attach a sentence with emotion and meaning it affects you and everyone around you.

Having words and emotional responses connected to those words at hand. Is a powerful way to counteract the effects of negative-limiting and restricting beliefs.

"The only thing that's keeping you from getting what you want is the story you kept telling yourself". —Tony Robbins

The lives we live are made up of our thoughts, beliefs, and feelings. At different times in life, we will all experience anxiety or uncertainty about aspects of it. That is a normal developmental part of being human. When for whatever reason we get stuck in those situations and are unable to find solutions to that situation.

Let's look at some words that will have the potential to change our lives.

Passionate   Transforming   Wellness   Worthy

Radiance   Renewal   Thriving   Purposeful

Energetic   Abundance   Align   Visionary

Creativity   Discovery   Love   Release

Peaceful   Growth   Imagination
Courageous

Serendipity   Grace   Harmonious   Visualize

Clarity   Focus   Persistence   Service

Faith   Prosperity   Insightful   Unlimited
Unleash

Results   Uncover   Solutions   Quality

Power/Powerful   Compelling   Exciting
Accomplish

Worthwhile   Succulent   Valued   Lovable

Loved   Loving   Believe   Self-confidence.   Deserving

Wealthy   Flourishing   Fortune

And write down.

Five you are familiar with and how that has influenced your life
....
....
....

Five that caused a negative reaction and a reason if you know.
....
....
....

Five that you would like to have in your life more.
....
....
....

It's interesting the words that we find negative as it may be the meaning, we have attached to them because of an event or incident.

That may be because of stories that we have been told by others.

You know we each have wounds that we have tried to make right in our lives.

Like we did not feel like we belonged or were approved of by others.

That may have caused us to have a belief that we were broken and until we fix ourselves, we cannot be accepted by others.

I believe we have always been whole and complete.

Our feelings have been hijacked by the opinions and control of others.

We'll rewrite the script of your life to focus on growth, self-love, and unlimited potential.

Understanding the beliefs and values that have shaped your reality.

Have you been living an empowered life up to now?

....
....
....

What beliefs or values have limited your reality?

....
....
....

Identify the beliefs and values that have held you back.

....
....
....

Do you understand the whys behind these beliefs and stories?

....

....

....

As we continue this journey, remember that you have the power to rewrite your story. By choosing empowering words and shedding limiting beliefs, you can create a new script for your life—one filled with love, growth, and boundless potential. Embrace your wholeness, and step into a brighter future.

When we start to acknowledge the power of words in shaping our realities. We can change our lives.

The Pollyanna Game

The Power of a Positive Attitude

In our journey through life, the way we perceive and respond to situations greatly influences our experiences. By adopting a positive and intentional attitude, we can transform our lives, building resilience and fostering a solutions-oriented mindset. This chapter delves into the profound impact of a positive attitude and resilience and introduces the Pollyanna Gratitude and Self-Appreciation Game—a practical tool to nurture these qualities.

A positive attitude is more than just a fleeting emotion; it is a sustained outlook that shapes how we interact with the world. It affects our mental and physical health, relationships, and overall life satisfaction.

It Improves our Mental Health, as a positive attitude reduces stress, anxiety, and depression. It promotes a sense of well-being and happiness, helping us navigate life's challenges with a clear and focused mind.

Our Relationships flourish more easily as positivity fosters better communication and deeper connections. It encourages empathy and understanding, strengthening our bonds with others.

It can often lead to greater success, with optimism and a can-do attitude propelling us towards our goals. They inspire perseverance and creativity, enabling us to overcome obstacles and achieve our dreams.

Importantly increases our resilience, studies have shown that a positive attitude builds resilience, the ability to bounce back from adversity. It equips us with the mental fortitude to handle setbacks and emerge stronger.

Resilience is the cornerstone of a fulfilling life. It is the capacity to recover quickly from difficulties and adapt to change. Resilient individuals are not immune to stress or adversity; rather, they possess the skills to manage and thrive despite challenges.

Here's how a positive attitude enhances our resilience.

Emotional Regulation

Positive emotions help us manage stress and maintain emotional balance. They provide a buffer against the negative effects of stress and promote a quicker recovery from adverse events. When we experience positive emotions, our bodies produce hormones like serotonin and dopamine, which counteract the effects of stress hormones like cortisol. This emotional balance enables us to remain calm and composed, even in the face of adversity, facilitating more effective problem-solving and decision

The Pollyanna Gratitude and Self-Appreciation Game

To cultivate a positive attitude and build resilience, it's important to engage in practices that reinforce these qualities. The Pollyanna Gratitude and Self-Appreciation Game is an excellent tool for this purpose. Inspired by the character Pollyanna, who always found something to be glad about, this game encourages us to focus on the positive aspects of our lives and ourselves.

This exercise is designed to illuminate the path of gratitude and self-appreciation, sparking the flame within you for personal growth. Just as Pollyanna found the good in every situation, let's explore the alphabet of your own positivity. Below are examples of each letter and why they could be perfect to begin the shift from negativity to positivity. As we know what we focus on grows and that is where our energy flows.

This exercise like many is simple and effective but not easy. Our minds are just wandering off and attracting negative, worrying, and limiting thoughts.

In retraining our minds – let's be gentle with ourselves. If we wander off, just start where you remembered and keep going.

There are several ways to play this game below is the Solo game.

You can go through the whole alphabet one letter at a time, reading and feeling into each one or you can pick three or four that resonate with you in that moment. Tune into the statement and the emotions it brings up.

Or you can use this statement with each letter

I am thankful .... And find something to be thankful for in that letter.

This is a good one to do in a group perhaps before a meeting or in a situation where people are not gelling well together. It is very useful if people are being negative, and the conversation is not being productive. It is useful while driving and younger people are in the car too. More interesting than counting horses or cows. I suggest two rounds with having to find a different item to be thankful for each time. Remember you cannot be holding a positive and negative thought at the same time.

I have used this many times. If I was getting anxious or overthinking it was a great way to distract me and bring me to a better place

Power statements are a great place to start.

These are the types of things that could be on a power statement.

What is the best that could happen today?

I make the best decisions for me.

It's easy for me to problem-solve.

Things just keep falling into place for me.

I can easily put things into perspective and understand that some things are for now, not forever.

I am lovable, loved, and loving.

My word is my bond, and I catch myself if on occasion I say something negative.

My word is my wand, and I am deliberately creating more joy and happiness for myself and others.

I am going to treat each day as a new beginning in my life.

This new beginning is just what I needed.

Finding a new job is easy for me and wouldn't take much time.

I am going to cherish all the moments of my life from now on.

Everything that I have dreamt of is about to begin.

I am open to new possibilities.

I am blessed to be a blessing.

The perfect person for me is right behind the corner!

I love taking care of my body. My body responds so beautifully to this care.

I deserve to be loved, just as I am.

I keep curiosity alive in my heart.

I am health, strength, peace, happiness, and prosperity rolled into one.

All my thoughts are positive and empowering.

I am full of empowering thoughts from the moment I wake up.

My ability to conquer my challenges is limitless.

I am enough and deserve more than enough.

I have the power to change my life by changing my thoughts.

I like the feeling of worthiness that is me.

It is all falling into place for me.

I am always going in the right direction for me.

I am love and I am the love that I seek.

He is looking for me.

I am already whole and complete.

We are two forks on the same plate.

All is well in my world.

I welcome this new season with calm confidence.

I am excited about how my life is going to change now.

I am worthy of a healthy loving relationship with a good person.

I embrace the future and everything my new life brings me.

I was meant to be here.

Things are getting better every day.

With passion and joy, I am creating my own future.

Whenever I need something, it manifests effortlessly into my life.

I am excited for this new beginning, and a new romantic page in my life!

I am ready to take up new adventures in life.

This year, I choose a path of happiness and wellness.

I am grateful for all I have and all that is to come.

Today, I support my body by moving it and growing strong.

I have the inner power and strength to deal with everything that comes my way.

I am willing to move in new directions, and I can learn what I need to know as I go.

I shall make some amazing friends as this new chapter begins.

I embrace all the great things that are about to come my way.

I celebrate the wins, big and small.

This is what a wealthy healthy woman looks like

I love my life; I love what I do, and I am flourishing

Life is so enjoyable for me now.

I have a wonderful supportive group of friends.

I travel easily and often.

I have met and am working with the best people for my business and my life.

Why a power statement? Is a great way to start changing how we see ourselves and how we feel about ourselves.

It is the beginning of creation. Now, the power statement is just one way that you can elevate your vibration and your frequency. Importantly, it helps you change the language that you are using to talk to yourself if we are going to be able to start making that shift from the old story to the new story. We start here. What we assign to ourselves internally makes all the difference of what happens in our life externally.

At the beginning, this will feel awkward. This will feel out of sync. It might not even feel true. I am encouraging you here at this moment to continue and set yourself up with a routine of using your power statement daily for at least 60 days.

We start our mornings from a place of empowerment and purpose. We are creating a new platform to live from.

Have your power statement in front as you stand in front of a mirror. You can write it down or have it on your phone . Posture is very important. For the right kind of energy coming into our bodies, and of course, our body is connected to our mind and our emotions. Get your posture right. Your head is above your shoulders. Make sure that you are standing up when in the mirror. This is where you can use the Magic Eye technique.

The Magic Eye technique is a technique that you can use to elevate your relationships. It is very good if you're having trouble connecting with people in your life. It helps you to hear when people are talking. And helps you to connect back to them.

By looking into someone's left eye, we trigger a natural bonding response in our brains, which can be used to build connections in various aspects of life, whether it's in personal relationships or professional interactions.

Your right eye is looking at the left eye and then as that interaction from the optic nerve is going around the brain it's impacting the amygdala where emotions come from, and it's creating this emotional resonance loop so that right eye to left eye contact is the most bonding eye contact you can have with someone.

Write a Power Statement for you!

Read it out loud. and importantly FEEL the words. Connect the statement with emotion. FEEL it as if you are the new you. It will become your new truth.

Your new narrative and story that you ARE living.

The Fairy Elephant Effect

When I was about 13, I went to the movies with my mum to watch "Any Which Way but Loose," starring Clint Eastwood. I was completely captivated by it. Something about the idea of driving a truck, being free on the open road, spoke to me. I remember turning to my mum afterwards, excited and full of possibility, and I said, "I want to be a truck driver!" Her response was quick and certain: "A girl doesn't do that." And just like that, my excitement deflated. I didn't realize it at the time, but her words planted a seed, a belief that there were things I couldn't or shouldn't do simply because I was a girl. It stayed with me at that moment. The world felt a little smaller after that.

Then, when I was around 16, I told my mum I wanted to be a vet. I loved animals, and it felt like a calling, something that would bring me purpose. But again, her response crushed me: "We can't afford it, and your grades are no good." It wasn't just about the money or the grades; it felt like she was telling me I wasn't enough. That my dreams were too big for me. I remember feeling helpless, like no matter what I wanted, there was always going to be some external force telling me I couldn't have it. It was as if her words wrapped around me, and I started believing that maybe she was right. Maybe I wasn't meant for more.

Years later, my first husband's words cut even deeper. I still remember the day he said, "You won't leave me because no one else would want you." It hit me like a punch to the gut. Those words lodged themselves deep inside, feeding on every insecurity I had. It wasn't just an insult—it was a belief he wanted me to internalize. And for a long time, I did. I let those words convince me I was unlovable, that I was stuck, that I didn't deserve better.

Looking back, I see how these moments shaped me, like invisible threads tightening around me, holding me back. It's like I became that Fairy Elephant with wings that were meant to fly, but every word, every belief someone else had about me weighed me down. It's hard to shake off those voices, but I'm beginning to realize that their words don't have to define me. It's a journey, but I'm learning to reclaim my own story, to write it on my terms.

K.H.

Discovering Self-Worth and Your Love Language

For what seemed a long time in my life, I felt trapped by a sense of powerlessness and unworthiness. These feelings stemmed from a belief system deeply ingrained by past experiences and societal expectations. I was always vigilant, living in fear that something bad was bound to happen and that, somehow, I deserved it. This mindset affected my relationships, leading me to prioritize being liked and needed over my own well-being. I often found myself becoming a "doormat," settling for less because I thought that was all I deserved.

The turning point came when I began exploring self-help literature, You Can Heal Your Life by Louise. L. Hay. Which I still refer tanything by Julia Cameron.

These books, among others, marked the beginning of a significant shift in my thinking.

For the first time, I started to understand the importance of knowing and valuing myself. It was only then that I allowed all of the unwanted and toxic thoughts and feelings to be acknowledged. In doing that I started to - with the help of ACC, a counselor, and belly dancing. Move past my past, letting it go, leaving it where it belonged. Behind me

Yes belly dancing, As it was allowed as part of my physical therapy. Which helped to release emotions and heal my body. This gave me the opportunity to meet and make some wonderful new friends.

Another book that influenced me was Gary Chapman's "Love Languages".

When I realized that my primary love languages were quality time and words of affirmation. This revelation helped me understand why I often felt misunderstood and why I had a deep-seated need for validation and connection.

Understanding my love languages explained so much about my past behavior. I had been labeled "needy" because I craved genuine quality time and meaningful interactions. Quality time, for me, meant more than just being in the same room as someone else; it meant engaging in undivided, meaningful conversations, and sharing moments that created a real connection. It wasn't about quantity but the quality.

"How you love yourself is how you teach others to love you."
— Rupi Kaur

Unlocking the Power of Love Languages

The Concept of Love Languages

Dr. Gary Chapman introduced the concept of love languages in his book, The 5 Love Languages: The Secret to Love that Lasts. According to Chapman, there are five primary ways people express and experience love. Understanding these can help you recognize how you and others prefer to give and receive love, leading to more fulfilling and harmonious relationships.

This was something that I found very useful in discovering how I heard love in my life, in my heart. It showed me why certain behaviors from others, had had a negative effect. In knowing what my love language was, it gave me knowledge that helped me see that I was not unappreciative or clingy or needy or demanding or nagging or angry or furious or upset or hurt or disappointed or feeling alone or feeling unloved or unlovable or not worthy of attention. I just hadn't had the right language activated in my life.

Below is a summary of The Five Love Languages

Words of Affirmation

Description: This love language uses words to affirm, appreciate, and encourage others.

Actions: Complimenting your partner, expressing gratitude, sending a thoughtful text, or offering words of encouragement.

Example: Telling your spouse, "I appreciate all the hard work you do," or sending an encouraging note to a friend.

Acts of Service

Description: For these people, actions speak louder than words. They feel loved when others do things for them.

Actions: Helping with household chores, running errands, or doing something special to make life easier for your loved one.

Example: Cooking dinner for your family or taking on a task your partner dislikes.

Receiving Gifts

Description: This love language is not about materialism but the thought and effort behind the gift.

Actions: Giving thoughtful gifts, remembering special occasions, and showing that you are thinking of the other person.

Example: Bringing home a small token of appreciation or making a handmade gift.

Quality Time

Description: This language is all about giving the other person your undivided attention.

Actions: Planning a special date, having meaningful conversations, or spending uninterrupted time together.

Example: Going on a walk together or having a device-free dinner to focus on each other.

Physical Touch

Description: Physical touch can range from holding hands to more intimate expressions of love.

Actions: Hugging, kissing, cuddling, or simply holding hands.

Example: Giving your partner a warm hug after a long day or patting your friend on the back.

Take the quiz overleaf to find your primary and secondary love languages.

Discover Your Love Language Quiz

No 1: I feel most loved when someone expresses their appreciation for me in words.
a) Always (Words of Affirmation)
b) Often
c) Sometimes
d) Rarely
e) Never

No 2: Doing things to help me (like chores or errands) makes me feel valued.
a) Always (Acts of Service)
b) Often
c) Sometimes
d) Rarely
e) Never

No 3: Receiving gifts from someone special makes me feel appreciated.
a) Always (Receiving Gifts)
b) Often
c) Sometimes
d) Rarely
e) Never

No 4: Spending uninterrupted, quality time with someone makes me feel important.
a) Always (Quality Time)
b) Often
c) Sometimes
d) Rarely
e) Never

No 5: I feel closest to someone when we hug, hold hands, or have physical contact.
a) Always (Physical Touch)
b) Often
c) Sometimes
d) Rarely
e) Never

No 6: Compliments and kind words mean a lot to me.
a) Always (Words of Affirmation)
b) Often
c) Sometimes
d) Rarely
e) Never

No 7: I appreciate when someone helps me out, especially when I'm busy or stressed.

a) Always (Acts of Service)
b) Often
c) Sometimes
d) Rarely
e) Never

No 8: Thoughtful gifts make me feel loved and cherished.
a) Always (Receiving Gifts)
b) Often
c) Sometimes
d) Rarely
e) Never

No 9: I feel special when someone makes time to just be with me.
a) Always (Quality Time)
b) Often
c) Sometimes
d) Rarely
e) Never

No 10: Physical signs of affection, like a pat on the back, make me feel connected.
a) Always (Physical Touch)
b) Often
c) Sometimes
d) Rarely
e) Never

No 11:
Hearing someone say they appreciate me makes my day.
a) Always (Words of Affirmation)
b) Often
c) Sometimes
d) Rarely
e) Never

No 12: I feel loved when someone helps me with something I need.
a) Always (Acts of Service)
b) Often
c) Sometimes
d) Rarely
e) Never

No 13: Getting a small gift unexpectedly makes me feel cared for.
a) Always (Receiving Gifts)
b) Often
c) Sometimes
d) Rarely
e) Never

No 14:
Quality time with someone I care about is the best way to show love.

a) Always (Quality Time)
b) Often
c) Sometimes
d) Rarely
e) Never

No 15: A hug or kiss from someone I love makes me feel secure.
a) Always (Physical Touch)
b) Often
c) Sometimes
d) Rarely
e) Never

Tally Up Your Results

For each section (1-15), assign points to your answers:

Always = 5 points
Often = 4 points
Sometimes = 3 points
Rarely = 2 points
Never = 1 point

Group the sections by love language and add up the points for each group:

Words of Affirmation: Sections 1, 6, 11
Acts of Service: Sections 2, 7, 12
Receiving Gifts: Sections 3, 8, 13
Quality Time: Sections 4, 9, 14
Physical Touch: Sections 5, 10, 15

The group with the highest total points represents your primary love language.

Example Tally

Words of Affirmation: 12 points
Acts of Service: 10 points
Receiving Gifts: 8 points
Quality Time: 11 points
Physical Touch: 14 points

In this example, Physical Touch is the primary love language since it has the highest total points.

Incorporate Your Love Languages into Your Daily Life

Incorporating love languages into your daily self-care routine can significantly enhance your well-being and self-love. Here's how you can activate and speak to yourself in each of the five love languages and we all know the more we know ourselves, the more understanding and compassionate we are with others. It starts with us and everything we do has an effect on our life. If we come from a place of love for us- consideration, no judgment, perfectly imperfectly us. Then life is immeasurably better for you and the ones you choose to be in your life with you.

Activating Your Top Two Love Languages for You and Only You

Once you have identified Your Top Two Love Languages

1. Words of Affirmation

Activities: Daily Affirmations: Start your day by looking in the mirror and speaking positive affirmations to yourself. Examples include "I am worthy," "I am capable," and "I love myself."

Journaling: Write down things you appreciate about yourself each day. Focus on your strengths, achievements, and positive qualities.

Actions: Positive Self-Talk: Throughout the day, replace negative thoughts with positive ones. If you make a mistake, remind yourself that you're learning and growing.

Compliment Yourself: Celebrate your successes, no matter how small. Acknowledge your effort and progress regularly.

2. Acts of Service

Activities: Organize Your Space: Dedicate time to clean and organize your living or working area. A tidy environment can reduce stress and increase your sense of accomplishment.

Prepare Healthy Meals: Cook nutritious meals for yourself. Consider this an act of love, nourishing your body with good food.

Actions: Plan Ahead: Set up a schedule or to-do list to make your life easier. Preparing for the next day the night before can help reduce anxiety and increase productivity.

Self-Care Routine: Develop a self-care routine that includes activities like exercising, meditating, or skincare. Consistently taking care of your physical and mental health is a powerful act of service to yourself.

3. Receiving Gifts

Activities: Treat Yourself: Buy something you've been wanting, whether it's a book, a piece of clothing, or a special treat. It doesn't have to be expensive; it just needs to bring you joy.

Create a Wish List: Keep a list of things you'd like to have or experiences you'd like to enjoy. Occasionally, reward yourself with something from the list.

Actions: Celebrate Milestones: Mark important achievements by gifting yourself something meaningful. It could be as simple as a favorite dessert or as elaborate as a weekend getaway.

Subscription Services: Sign up for a subscription service that delivers something you enjoy regularly, like a book club, beauty box, or gourmet snacks.

4. Quality Time

Alone Time: Schedule regular alone time where you engage in activities you love, such as reading, painting, or taking long walks.

Mindfulness Practice: Dedicate time to mindfulness practices like meditation or yoga to connect with yourself deeply.

Actions: Digital Detox: Take breaks from digital devices to spend quality time with yourself. Use this time to reflect, relax, and rejuvenate.

Hobbies: Engage in hobbies that you are passionate about. This can include anything from gardening to playing a musical instrument, allowing you to immerse yourself fully in what you enjoy.

5. Physical Touch

Activities: Self-Massage: Learn simple self-massage techniques or use tools like a foam roller to relieve tension in your body.

Comforting Touch: Wrap yourself in a cozy blanket, take a warm bath, or use a weighted blanket to provide comfort and relaxation.

Actions: Exercise Engage in physical activities like yoga, stretching, or dancing. Physical movement can help you connect with your body and feel more grounded.

Skincare Routine: Develop a nurturing skincare routine, paying attention to how each product feels on your skin. This can be a soothing way to show love to your body.

By incorporating these activities, actions, and thoughts into your daily life, you can actively practice self-love in a manner aligned with your personal love language. This not only boosts your self-esteem but also enhances your overall emotional and mental well-being.

Some combinations of love languages with others

For Words of Affirmation and Quality Time: Schedule regular time for heartfelt conversations with your partner and friends. Compliment and affirm their qualities and actions sincerely.

Combine Acts of service with Physical touch. For example, help your partner with a chore and then relax together with a comforting touch.

Transforming Your Interactions

Once you know your love language, and those of the people around you, you can tailor your interactions to make them feel more loved and appreciated.

Here's how:

With Your Partner: Understand how they express love and what makes them feel loved. If they value quality time, prioritize undistracted moments together.

With Your Children: Recognize their unique love languages and express love in ways that resonate with them. For example, if they prefer physical touch, offer more hugs and physical affection.

With Coworkers: Understanding their love languages can improve workplace harmony. If a colleague values words of affirmation, offer genuine compliments and recognition for their hard work.

With Your Boss: Tailor your appreciation in ways that align with their love language. If they appreciate acts of service, go the extra mile to support their projects.

By learning and applying the love languages, you can create stronger, more positive connections in every area of your life. Understanding how others receive love allows you to communicate more effectively, reduce misunderstandings, and build a more supportive and loving environment. And of course, you have a more complete blueprint of yourself.

Reflection Questions and Action Steps

What is important and vital for you to be the best and better version of yourself?

Write down 5 things

....
....
....
....
....

Reflect on Your Own Love Language:

How does knowing your love language change your perspective on past interactions?

....
....
....

Observe Others: Pay attention to how your loved ones express love and respond to different gestures.

Communicate: Share your love language with others and ask about theirs. This opens a dialogue that can enhance mutual understanding and respect.

Practice: Make a conscious effort to use the love languages in your daily interactions. Notice the impact this has on your relationships.

Embracing the concept of love languages is a journey toward deeper self-awareness and more meaningful connections. It's a tool that can transform not just your relationships but your entire approach to communicating and understanding the people around you. As we are discovering with making the effort to know and understand ourselves, by letting go of the past and becoming more accepting of where we end and others begin, life opens up for us in wondrous ways.

"We are the way. It all starts and ends with Us"
— Elysabeth Wolter

Loving and appreciating ourselves is a transformative practice that shapes how we interact with the world. By activating your love language internally, you can cultivate a deeper sense of self-worth and happiness. This self-love not only improves your relationship with yourself but also enhances how you feel in your interactions and experiences.

When you affirm yourself with kind words, you start believing in your own worth and capabilities. Acts of service directed towards yourself remind you that your needs and well-being are important. Receiving gifts from yourself, whether tangible or intangible, reinforces that you deserve to be treated with care and thoughtfulness. Spending quality time with yourself fosters a deeper understanding and appreciation of who you are. Physical touch, even when self-administered, can soothe and reassure you, making you feel more grounded and loved.

The more you nurture self-love through these practices, the more you will notice a positive shift in your interactions with others and the world around you. People often respond to the energy we emit; when we love and appreciate ourselves, we attract similar energy from others. This reciprocal relationship can create a cycle of positivity, enhancing both our internal and external worlds.

Starting a self-love journey through your love language is a personal and empowering experience. It allows you to take control of your emotional well-being and fosters a healthier, more loving relationship with yourself. As you continue to practice self-love, you'll find that the world often reflects that love and appreciation back to you, creating a more fulfilling and joyful life.

"One of the best guides to how to be self-loving is to give ourselves the love we are often dreaming about receiving from others." — bell hooks

Recording Achievements

Make a gratitude jar, when anything good happens in your life. Write it down and put it in the jar. This helps you maintain a list of your accomplishments, big and small. Retraining your mind and emotions to look for the good and importantly if you are having one of those days -because it does happen. you may be feeling flat or uninspired or that nothing seems to be happening. Take out some of those notes and read them, it really helps to change your perspective and attitude and often that is all you need.

The Unseen Ripples of Rejection

"Being yourself means shedding all the layers of looking good, wanting to be liked, being scared to stand out, and trying to be who you think people want you to be."
— Jeff Moore

Fear of rejection is a pervasive and insidious force, often manifesting in subtle yet impact ways. It whispers that our creations, ideas, or expressions aren't good enough and convinces us to hide them away from the world. For me, this fear materialized in the form of poetry. Over the years, I poured my heart and soul into writing hundreds of poems, each a reflection of my thoughts, emotions, and experiences. Yet, instead of sharing these pieces of myself, I stored them in a drawer, hidden from view. The fear of rejection told me, "There's no point in sharing; no one will understand or appreciate them."

This attitude of "there's no point" is a protective mechanism, shielding us from potential criticism, judgment, or disapproval. It can stifle creativity, hinder growth, and prevent us from fully expressing ourselves. The thought of exposing my innermost thoughts and feelings to others felt overwhelming. What if they didn't resonate? What if they rejected not just my work, but me as a person?

But what about you?

Has fear of rejection led you to abandon a passion or talent?

Has it made you question your worth or value?

Fear of rejection is a shared human experience that affects each of us in unique ways. It can manifest as hesitation to pursue a dream, reluctance to voice an opinion or avoidance of new opportunities.

The first step in overcoming this fear is acknowledging its presence and understanding its impact.

What have you liked to do, but put aside?

....

....

....

"Be who you are and say what you feel, because those who mind don't matter and those who matter don't mind."
— Dr Seuss

Your Wonderful Life

When we start moving towards living by design, it's important to remember that manifesting is not something separate from us. We are manifestations of creation itself, and every day we are creating. The challenge is that many of us are creating by accident rather than by design. The next exercise will stretch you, as we are not used to being ignited by our imagination. Albert Einstein said creation happens twice—first in our mind, then in reality. How we see and feel about a situation creates a ripple effect. So when you do this exercise, it's not about restrictions or reality. It's about connection and allowing your imagination to expand beyond the ceilings you've created.

I encourage you to do this exercise regularly, once or twice a week. It does more than just let you imagine a perfect day. It reignites your ability to dream and reveals your aspirations. Sometimes, these aspirations have been dimmed or hidden away. This exercise is a way to turn the switch back on. If you've been doing morning pages, this will complement them. Every exercise I share is helping you tune into your inner voice. You're creating a relationship with yourself—the likable, lovable you, waiting to be recognized.

This exercise, practiced regularly, will create pivotal moments. In my own life, I've experienced more than one of these magical days.

Find a comfortable place, somewhere safe and cozy. Lie down or sit, as long as you won't be interrupted. Start by imagining your perfect day.

What does your bed feel like? Is it comfortable? How do the sheets feel against your skin? Who are you waking up next to? A partner, children, a pet, or just yourself? Remember, we're only imagining the good stuff here. When you wake up feeling good, how does your body feel? Are you tuned into it, thanking it for being amazing? Now, imagine getting out of bed. What are the first things you're going to do in the next two hours? Will you have coffee, meditate, write your morning pages, go for a run, stretch, or shower?

Think about the rest of your morning. What kind of work are you doing? Are you working from home or going to an office? What does it look like, and how are you connecting with the people around you? What did you have for lunch? Were you alone or with others? How was the conversation, and how did the food make you feel?

How are you spending your afternoon? Who are you with? How does your energy feel as the day continues? When you're heading home, reflect on how you feel about your day. Was it purposeful and pleasurable? Do you feel satisfied? In this perfect day, how do you feel as the day winds down? Are you going out for dinner, spending quality time with loved ones, or learning something new?

Now, imagine hopping into bed. How do you feel at the end of this perfect day? What are your thoughts as you prepare for sleep?

Next, expand this to your perfect week. What happens on each day? Have you caught up with relatives, traveled, or felt fully engaged with life? How does your body feel? What are you eating? Who are you talking to? What kind of conversations are you having? What are you learning? What are you reading?

Then, think about your perfect month. What does that look like? You can continue this exercise for a perfect year, but let's focus on a day, a week, and a month for now. Write down how you feel, what it looks like, and who is there with you.

When I started this exercise, it was just a way to break free from my limitations and the ceilings I had put in place. But over time, I've had perfect days, perfect weeks, and I'm now entering perfect months. It hasn't taken long, and it's a beautiful way to give yourself permission to think and feel differently about the life you're going to lead. I encourage you to do this regularly. You matter, and you are worth it.

Breadcrumbs and New Destinations

Things stick and it can take us a while to move those beliefs out and the first step is allowing ourselves to think differently. And my handwriting is still atrocious at times, lol and I don't care. It is just a by-product of the environment I grew up in.

And I ACCEPT that as part of who I am, and I am enough.

It is no longer an issue for me and if others do not approve, well what others think about me is NONE OF MY BUSINESS.

Read that again What others think about me is NONE OF MY BUSINESS

And what others think about you IS NONE OF YOUR BUSINESS too.

This way of Being you can feel very foreign and slightly ridiculous - I know right?

We want others to love and approve of us and if we don't have other people's validation, acceptance.

How will we be qualifying our existence.?

How are we going to be acknowledged?

How will we know if we fit in?

Where will we be accepted?

Where are we seen as having value?

How will we be included?

This can't be right, right?

"IT IS A PARADOX. THE LESS YOU NEED SOMEONE'S APPROVAL, THE MORE YOU ARE ABLE TO LOVE THEM."
—Susan Jeffers, *Feel the Fear and Do It Anyway*

Take a few moments to write down anything that may come up from those questions

_____
_____
_____
_____
_____

Time to start finding your breadcrumbs — that is your unique path to becoming the version of you that you like and love the best.

"Everybody talks about wanting to change things and help and fix, but ultimately all you can do is fix yourself. And that's a lot. Because if you can fix yourself, it has a ripple effect." — Rob Reiner

Unveiling the Layers of Self

"Believing in our hearts that who we are is enough is the key to a more satisfying and balanced life." — Ellen Sue Stern

Uncovering the layers of our identity is a journey that can span a lifetime. We are complex beings, shaped by our experiences, beliefs, and emotions. As we grow and evolve, we continuously discover new facets of ourselves, revealing deeper truths and understanding. This process is not linear; it is an ever-changing exploration that requires patience, self-compassion, and a willingness to face uncomfortable truths.

Each moment of self-awareness is an opportunity for healing. When we recognize a situation, pattern, or belief that no longer serves us, we begin to mend the fractures within. These moments of realization are powerful; they are the catalysts for transformation. You Matter—these two simple words hold immense power. They remind us that our experiences, thoughts, and emotions are valid and that we have always been.

In the journey of self-discovery, we often encounter memories or emotions that are difficult to process. For me, one such memory was the "Butter Dish Incident." This seemingly trivial event held a significant emotional charge, representing a deeper wound of not feeling enough. During an Aaron Doughty meditation on forgiveness, I revisited this memory and the emotions it carried. The hurt, disappointment, and sense of worthlessness resurfaced, revealing the depth of the pain I had buried.

As I delved deeper into the meditation, I began to see the situation from a new perspective. It was as if I had stepped outside my body, viewing the scene from an expanded state of consciousness. I saw my mother not just as the source of my pain, but as a woman struggling with her own demons. Her actions, which had caused me so much hurt, were a reflection of her internal turmoil, not a judgment of my worth.

This realization was a turning point. It allowed me to see beyond the immediate pain and recognize the interconnectedness of our experiences. We are more than the sum of our experiences; we are energetic beings capable of profound growth and healing. In that moment, I felt compassion for my mother, understanding her struggles and acknowledging her humanity. It was a powerful experience that shifted my perception and allowed me to forgive her.

In writing this book, I honor my mother and all the mothers who have endured similar struggles. They lived in a time when societal expectations were rigid, and opportunities for self-expression were limited. My mother was a bright and beautiful woman, trapped by the constraints of her time. She wanted to learn and grow, but the societal norms of the era kept her confined to a life she did not choose.

My mother's life was marked by hardship. She was a wife to a traveling salesman, often left alone to care for her children and manage the household. She did not drive, had limited resources, and faced many challenges. Despite these struggles, she pursued education, achieving school certifications in English and Māori. Her life was a testament to resilience, yet she remained trapped by the societal expectations of her time.

Upon her death, I discovered her written thoughts and regrets. She expressed a deep desire for better relationships with her children yet felt incapable of achieving them. This realization was heartbreaking, as it revealed the depth of her emotional pain. My mother never reconciled with her past or made peace with her emotions. Her struggles with depression and anxiety were palpable, yet she remained silent, unable to move past her pain.

This book is for all the people who find themselves trapped by their past, for all the mothers who struggled in silence, and for anyone seeking healing and growth. The information available today offers new possibilities. You have the power to break patterns, to choose differently, and to create a life aligned with your true self. Persistent and consistent actions are key to achieving lasting change. Remember, we are never static; we are energy in motion, capable of transcending our past and embracing our potential.

As you read this book, may you find the courage to face your fears, the strength to heal your wounds, and the wisdom to embrace your true self. You matter, and your journey is worth every step.

Use the space below to record any thoughts or emotions from this chapter

Did it sound like something present in your life?

Do you know people like that?

Have you been trapped in societal norms?

....
....
....

If so, what were they or are they?

....
....
....

The Fairy Elephant Effect

My heart used to sink when, in response to what I thought was a brilliant idea, I'd hear things like, "Well, that won't work," or "If it were such a great idea, someone would've done it by now." I was young, brimming with ideas, but over time, I stopped speaking them out loud. Eventually, I stopped dreaming altogether.

The adults in my life probably thought they were shielding me from disappointment and disaster, but all I internalized was the message: "Get your head out of the clouds and face reality."

The kicker? I know I've inherited some of that 'dream-killing' language myself. I've probably passed on that negativity without even realizing it. I think back on moments where my words may have dampened someone else's spark.

But now, I'm here to say—whether you're young or old—never stop dreaming. No matter what anyone has told you, it's never too late to embrace your ideas, your imagination, and your vision.

L.F.

This is part of my own Fairy Elephant Effect: recognizing those moments where I let others squash my dreams and finding the courage to reclaim them. You can do it too. Don't let the voices of the past keep you from the future you can still create. Keep dreaming. Keep believing.

The Power of Language

The power of language and its role in transforming our lives reads like a road map for meaningful change. By exploring how our words, beliefs, and emotions create our reality, you offer readers both insight and practical tools for rewriting their narratives. Below is an interactive script that includes the key ideas you've shared, engaging quotes, and a list of transformative words, designed to evoke reflection and action.

The script of our lives is often authored by the beliefs, values, and stories we've accumulated over time. But what if those stories no longer serve us? What if the beliefs holding us back are outdated, inaccurate, or inherited from someone else's narrative? We possess the power to rewrite our story, to craft a new reality by transforming our thoughts, beliefs, and the words we use.

Yet, many of us continue to recycle the same old stories, hoping for new outcomes. We speak the same sentences to ourselves and others, unaware of their influence on our emotions, actions, and bodies. If your thoughts are filled with fear or doubt, they manifest in your language, affecting your body and your world.

The Connection Between Words and Well-Being

Our words are more than just sounds—they are powerful reflections of our inner world. They shape our reality, for better or worse. When we attach emotion and meaning to our words, we not only affect ourselves, but we also influence those around us.

Consider this: If you repeatedly tell yourself, "I'm not good enough," or "I never have enough money," these statements anchor you to a reality where these thoughts are true. Over time, these words shape your mindset, and your actions—or lack thereof—follow suit. Negative self-talk perpetuates a cycle of negativity, making it difficult to move forward or feel empowered.

In contrast, by consciously choosing new words—words that uplift, energize, and inspire—you begin to open new doors. You start creating a new narrative, one filled with possibilities instead of limitations. As the gatekeeper of your thoughts, you have the power to shift your perspective and, by extension, your entire life.

"Change your thoughts, and you change your world."
— Norman Vincent Peale

A New Narrative

So, where do we begin? Let's start by embracing the idea that we have the power to choose our words with intention. Language is a portal to transformation. By filling our minds and hearts with words that reflect the life we desire, we can gradually shift our internal dialogue and, eventually, our external reality.

We can use techniques such as:

Challenging limiting beliefs

Practicing positive affirmations

Visualization

EFT tapping

Mindfulness

power statements

Morning pages

These practices have the potential to rewrite our narrative, leading to greater contentment, inner peace, and reduced stress. The key is to remember that our words are not passive—they actively shape our experience. By changing your internal and external language, you gain the greatest influence over your life.

Imagine saying, "I am worthy of abundance," instead of, "I can never get ahead." Notice how your body responds when you make that shift. Your posture changes. You feel more empowered, hopeful, and energized.

As you introduce these new words into your life, you begin to fill your glass with fresh perspectives and emotions that support your highest aspirations. When you stop focusing on the problem and instead focus on the solution, you open yourself to new opportunities.

Transformative Words for a New Reality

Here are some words that have the potential to change your life. Spend time reflecting on them and incorporating them into your daily language:

Passionate	Persistence
Transforming	Service
Wellness	Faith
Worthy	Prosperity
Radiance	Insightful
Renewal	Unlimited
Thriving	Unleash
Purposeful	Results
Energetic	Uncover
Abundance	Solutions
Align	Quality
Visionary	Power/Powerful
Creativity	Compelling
Discovery	Exciting
Love	Accomplish
Release	Worthwhile
Peaceful	Succulent
Growth	Valued
Imagination	Loveable
Courageous	Loved
Serendipity	Loving
Grace	Believe
Harmonious	Self-confidence
Visualize	Deserving
Clarity	Wealthy
Focus	Flourishing
	Fortune

Consider writing these words in a journal and reflecting on how they resonate with you. Which ones feel true?

....
....
....

Which ones challenge you?

....
....
....

How can you begin to incorporate these words into your daily thoughts and actions?

....
....
....

"You are the author of your own story. Write wisely."
— Anonymous

Interactive Exercise

Take a few moments to reflect on the following questions

What are the limiting beliefs or stories you've been telling yourself?

....
....
....
....
....

How have these stories shaped your actions and experiences?

....
....
....
....
....

Choose three words from the list above that resonate with you. Write them down and consider how you can begin to incorporate them into your life. How will they feel and or in what kind of sentence or situations?

_____
_____
_____
_____
_____

Practice speaking these words out loud with emotion and intention. Notice how your energy shifts when you affirm these positive words.

By changing the words we use, we start to shift our reality. We move from a space of survival into one of thriving, from disempowerment to empowerment. Our language becomes the gateway to a new narrative—one where we choose to live a life of purpose, passion, and possibility.

"Words are the most powerful force available to humanity. We can choose to use this force constructively with words of encouragement, or destructively with words of despair.

Words have energy and power with the ability to help, heal, hinder, hurt, harm, humiliate, and humble." — Yehuda Berg

The choice is yours. What story will you write next?

Let's look at the double meaning and emotional imprint for words here are some examples below.

The Word "Precious"

Let's explore "precious" in two different contexts:

Positive Example: Treasuring Something Valuable

Conversation:

A friend hands you a family heirloom and says, "This necklace is precious to me. It has been in my family for generations."

Emotional Meaning:

Here, "precious" is infused with a sense of value, care, and love. The word implies that the item is cherished and deeply meaningful. When we use "precious" in this way, we communicate gratitude, respect, and emotional connection to something or someone.

Outcome:

This use of the word creates a feeling of warmth and reverence. The person receiving the necklace would likely feel honored and entrusted with something important. This establishes a bond and fosters positive emotions.

Negative Example: Overly Sensitive or Demanding

Conversation:

Someone at work refers to a colleague, saying, "Oh, don't bother her with that. She's too precious to handle any real stress."

Emotional Meaning:

In this context, "precious" has a negative connotation. It suggests that the person is overly sensitive, fragile, or high-maintenance, implying that they are not resilient or capable. This usage undermines the person's credibility and can create distance or resentment.

Outcome:

This use of the word subtly diminishes the person being spoken about. It could lead to the individual being excluded or not taken seriously, affecting their confidence and how others view them.

Example 2: "Failure" vs. "Learning Experience"

Failure as Final

Conversation:

"I didn't get the promotion. I guess I'm just a failure."

Emotional Meaning:

Here, "failure" is seen as a label that defines the person. The word carries a sense of shame, inadequacy, and finality. By identifying oneself as a failure, the person shuts down possibilities for growth and improvement.

Outcome:

Using "failure" in this way can lead to feelings of defeat, low self-worth, and a lack of motivation to try again. It creates a self-fulfilling prophecy where the person stops seeking new opportunities because they believe they are incapable of success.

Failure as a Learning Experience

Conversation:

"I didn't get the promotion, but I learned a lot from the interview process. Next time, I'll be even more prepared."

Emotional Meaning:

Here, the experience is reframed as a valuable lesson. The person acknowledges the setback but sees it as part of a larger journey toward success. The focus is on growth, learning, and persistence.

Outcome:

This perspective encourages resilience and self-confidence. The person is more likely to bounce back, seek new opportunities, and eventually achieve their goals. The language opens the door to future possibilities.

Example 3: "Busy" vs. "purposeful"

Busy as Overwhelmed

Conversation:

"I'm just so busy. I have too much on my plate, and I can't seem to keep up."

Emotional Meaning:

"Busy" in this context implies a sense of overwhelm, stress, and lack of control. It often carries a negative connotation that the person is overextended and perhaps inefficient. There is no pride or purpose attached to the word—just exhaustion.

Outcome:

This framing can lead to burnout and a sense of futility. The word "busy" suggests that the person is constantly reacting to demands rather than intentionally managing their time or energy. It leaves little room for fulfillment or satisfaction.

Purposeful as Intentional and Fulfilled

Conversation:

"I've had a productive day. I focused on my top priorities and made real progress."

Emotional Meaning:

Here, "purposeful" suggests that the person is in control of their time and actions. It implies that they have been purposeful and successful in achieving meaningful outcomes. The word carries a sense of accomplishment and satisfaction.

Outcome:

This use of language empowers the person. It reinforces the idea that they are capable of managing their workload effectively and can celebrate their achievements. This mindset promotes continued focus and motivation.

Example 4: "Challenge" vs. "Opportunity"

Challenge as a Barrier

Conversation:

"This project is going to be a real challenge. I'm not sure how I'm going to get through it."

Emotional Meaning:

The word "challenge" can be perceived as a hurdle, something difficult and possibly insurmountable. It brings with it a feeling of struggle and doubt.

Outcome:

By framing the situation as a challenge, the person might feel daunted and anxious about what lies ahead. It creates a sense of resistance and uncertainty, making it harder to approach the task with confidence.

Opportunity as a Positive Shift

Conversation:

"This project is a great opportunity to showcase my skills and take on new responsibilities."

Emotional Meaning:

The word "opportunity" reframes the same situation in a positive light. It suggests possibility, growth, and potential success. The emotional tone shifts from fear to excitement and anticipation.

Outcome:

This perspective creates momentum. The person feels more optimistic and energized, ready to take on the task with a sense of purpose and enthusiasm. It promotes a can-do attitude that increases the likelihood of success.

Example 5: "Sacrifice" vs. "Investment"

Sacrifice as Loss

Conversation:

"I'm making a lot of sacrifices for my career. I don't have time for myself or my family."

Emotional Meaning:

The word "sacrifice" often carries a heavy emotional burden, implying loss, deprivation, and perhaps resentment. It suggests that something valuable is being given up, leading to a feeling of imbalance or hardship.

Outcome:

This framing can lead to burnout, dissatisfaction, and frustration. It sets the stage for feelings of regret or a sense of futility in pursuing one's goals. The focus is on what is lost rather than what is gained.

Investment as Purposeful Effort

Conversation:

"I'm investing time and energy into my career right now because I know it will pay off in the long run."

Emotional Meaning:

The word "investment" conveys a sense of purpose, intentionality, and future reward. It implies that the effort being put in is worthwhile and that there will be positive outcomes as a result.

Outcome:

This perspective fosters a sense of motivation and commitment. The person feels that their efforts are valuable and will lead to growth, success, or fulfillment. It shifts the focus from present struggles to future rewards.

Conclusion: The Power of Reframing Language

As we see in these examples, the language we use has a profound effect on how we perceive ourselves, our challenges, and our opportunities. The emotional meaning attached to words can either lift us up or hold us back. When we choose words that empower us, we set ourselves up for success. By being intentional with our language, we can shift our mindset, influence our emotions, and create a more fulfilling life.

Ultimately, the key is to be mindful of the words we use, not only with others but with ourselves. Words like "opportunity," "growth," "learning," and "investment" carry a positive emotional charge, while words like "failure," "busy," and "sacrifice" can drain our energy. By consciously choosing words that reflect our desired reality, we open ourselves to new possibilities and set the stage for personal transformation.

The impact of words, especially when delivered with emotion and authority, is central to the Fairy Elephant Effect. Often, it's not just what is said, but how it's said and the emotional energy behind it that shapes our perception and experience.

Take a moment to reflect on the words that have left a lasting impression on you, particularly those that have had a less-than-desirable effect. They might have been spoken by someone in a position of authority—a teacher, a parent, a boss—or even by yourself in moments of doubt. These words may carry emotional weight that has shaped your beliefs and actions over time.

Here's a simple exercise:

Take 5 minutes to think about any specific words or phrases that have impacted you negatively.

Write them down, noting how they made you feel and the emotional connotation they carried (e.g., "failure" made me feel inadequate, "sensitive" made me feel weak).

Reflect on why these words stuck with you—was it the emotion behind them? The person who said them? The context in which they were said?

Once you've identified these words, recognize their impact, and remember that you have the power to change the script. By becoming aware of the influence these words have had on you, you can begin to rewrite your narrative and replace them with words that empower and uplift you.

EFT Tapping: A Path to Freedom

EFT tapping is something I hold dear to my heart. It has been the key to moving past complex post-traumatic stress disorder, severe anxiety, panic attacks, and depression. I struggled with low confidence and self-esteem—trapped by those life-stealing emotions. And the greatest of these is fear. Fear held me captive for so long, keeping me stuck in patterns I didn't even recognize at the time.

When you're caught in that low, negative energy, you start to think in ways that aren't truly your own. You may feel jealousy or envy, pass judgment on others, or focus on external problems instead of working on yourself. But here's the truth: EFT is an incredibly powerful tool for change. While you cannot erase the events or situations of your past, you can remove the emotional charge attached to them. And that, my friends, is true freedom.

By releasing those emotions, the past remains in the past, and you finally give yourself permission to live in peace. Fear no longer rules your life, and those negative emotions take a permanent vacation. EFT changed my life, and it can change yours too.

In this chapter, you'll find tapping scripts that helped me on my journey. I'll also introduce you to some alternative tapping points, explain a bit about Chinese medicine, and suggest people you can check out for further learning. This is the beginning of your own transformation, just as it was for me.

EFT (Emotional Freedom Techniques) tapping can change your emotional state by combining elements of cognitive therapy with physical stimulation of specific acupuncture points, which are believed to help balance the body's energy system. Here's how EFT works to shift emotions:

1. Acupressure and Energy Flow

Tapping on Meridians: EFT involves tapping on specific meridian points on the body, which are part of the traditional Chinese medicine system. These points are believed to be channels through which the body's energy flows. When the energy is blocked or disrupted, it can result in emotional or physical distress.

By tapping on these points, EFT helps to unblock or rebalance this energy, leading to an emotional release or shift.

2. Cognitive Shift

Exposure and Cognitive Reframing: EFT combines tapping with the focus on a specific negative emotion, memory, or belief. By acknowledging and verbalizing the issue while tapping, individuals can process the emotion more effectively. This process often leads to cognitive reframing, where the negative thought or belief is transformed into a more neutral or positive one.

3. Reduction of Stress Response

Calming the Nervous System: Tapping on these meridian points has been shown to reduce the body's stress response by lowering cortisol levels. Cortisol is a hormone released in response to stress, and elevated levels can exacerbate emotional distress. By calming the nervous system through tapping, EFT helps to bring the body back into a state of relaxation, making it easier to shift out of a negative emotional state.

4. Mind-Body Connection

Physical and Emotional Integration: EFT taps into the mind-body connection, recognizing that emotions are not just mental but also physical. By addressing both aspects simultaneously—thinking about the emotion and tapping on the body—EFT helps integrate the emotional experience, leading to a more profound and lasting change in the emotional state.

5. Empowerment and Self-Regulation

Taking Control: EFT empowers individuals to take control of their emotional well-being. The technique is simple and can be practiced independently, allowing people to regulate their emotions whenever they need. This sense of empowerment contributes to an overall positive shift in emotional state.

In summary, EFT tapping changes your emotional state by balancing energy flow, reframing negative thoughts, reducing stress, integrating the mind and body, and empowering self-regulation. This holistic approach helps release emotional blocks, leading to a more balanced and positive emotional state.

The SUDS (Subjective Units of Distress Scale) is a tool used in EFT (Emotional Freedom Techniques) and other therapeutic practices to measure the intensity of a person's emotional distress or discomfort in relation to a specific issue. It allows individuals to quantify their feelings on a scale, making it easier to assess changes in emotional states throughout the tapping process.

The SUDS (Subjective Units of Distress Scale) is a tool used in EFT (Emotional Freedom Techniques) and other therapeutic practices to measure the intensity of a person's emotional distress or discomfort in relation to a specific issue. It allows individuals to quantify their feelings on a scale, making it easier to assess changes in emotional states throughout the tapping process.

How SUDS Works Identifying the Issue

Before starting EFT, the individual identifies a specific issue, emotion, or memory they want to address.

Rating the Intensity. The person rates their level of distress on a scale from 0 to 10, where:

0 indicates no distress or discomfort.

10 represents the highest level of distress imaginable.

This initial rating is the baseline SUDS level.

Tapping Process

The individual then engages in EFT tapping, focusing on the identified issue while tapping on specific meridian points on the body.

Reassessing the SUDS Level

After a round of tapping, the person reassesses their level of distress using the SUDS scale.

The goal is to notice a reduction in the SUDS score, indicating a decrease in emotional intensity.

Repeating as Needed

The process is repeated, with additional rounds of tapping and reassessment, until the SUDS level is ideally reduced to 0 or a significantly lower number.

Why SUDS is Important in EFT:

Quantifiable Progress: SUDS provides a way to measure progress in real-time. By tracking changes in SUDS levels, individuals and practitioners can see how effective the EFT tapping is in reducing emotional distress.

The SUDS scale is subjective, meaning it reflects the individual's personal experience. This makes it a highly personalized tool that captures how the person is truly feeling at each stage.

If the SUDS level doesn't decrease as expected, it may indicate the need to explore deeper or related issues, adjust the tapping script, or address resistance to change.

In summary, SUDS is a simple but powerful tool used in EFT to help individuals track the intensity of their emotional distress, providing clear feedback on the effectiveness of the tapping process.

0 indicates no distress or discomfort.

10 represents the highest level of distress imaginable.

This initial rating is the baseline SUDS level.

Tapping Process. The individual then engages in EFT tapping, focusing on the identified issue while tapping on specific meridian points on the body.

The goal is to notice a reduction in the SUDS score, indicating a decrease in emotional intensity.

EFT Tapping for Letting Go of Overthinking

Assessing the Overthinking with SUDS

Identify the Overthinking: Think about a situation or thought pattern where you find yourself overthinking.

Rate the Intensity: On a scale of 0 to 10, where 0 is no overthinking and 10 is overwhelming overthinking, rate your current level of distress.

Tapping Points

Setup Statement (Karate Chop Point):

While tapping on the Karate Chop point (side of the hand), repeat the following three times: Even though I am always overthinking – I deeply and completely love, honor, and accept myself

Go through the tapping points and then access the suds score

Tap again using either the same phrase or a phrase like Even though -I often overthink — I deeply and completely love, honor, and accept myself

Repeating any phase/ phrases that resonated with your specific experience of overthinking or modifying them as needed.

Reassessing the SUDS Level

After one or two rounds of tapping, pause and reassess your SUDS level. Has the intensity of your overthinking decreased? If not, continue tapping through the points until you feel a noticeable reduction.

You can adjust the statement if needed again like these:

"Even though I still have some overthinking I deeply and completely love, honor, and accept myself."

"Even though I'm not completely free of these thoughts. I deeply and completely love, honor, and accept myself."

"Even though I sometimes doubt the process that things can work out for me. I deeply and completely love, honor, and accept myself."

After this final round, reassess your SUDS level. Ideally, your distress around overthinking should be significantly lower, and you should feel more aligned with the belief that things are working out for you.

Consistency: Practise this tapping sequence regularly to reinforce the belief that things are working out for you and to ease the habit of overthinking.

This EFT tapping sequence aims to help you release the habit of overthinking and cultivate a mindset of trust and positivity, knowing that things are indeed working out in your favor.

When using the SUDS (Subjective Units of Distress Scale) in EFT (Emotional Freedom Techniques), the primary focus is usually on reducing negative emotions or distress. However, at the other end of the scale, EFT can also be used to elevate positive emotions and enhance positive beliefs by "flipping" the focus of the process. This approach is sometimes referred to as "tapping in" positive emotions or affirmations.

How SUDS Can Be Used to Elevate Emotional State

Instead of focusing on distress, the individual identifies a positive emotional state or belief they want to enhance, such as joy, confidence, gratitude, or a specific empowering belief.

Rating the Positive Emotion

The person uses the SUDS scale to assess their current level of this positive emotion or belief, where:

0 might represent the absence of the desired positive emotion (e.g., "I don't feel confident at all").

10 represents the highest level of the desired emotion (e.g., "I feel completely confident").

Impressing Positive Statements

The individual taps on the same meridian points while focusing on positive affirmations or statements that resonate with their desired emotional state.

Examples might include:

"I deeply and completely accept myself."

"I am confident and capable."

"I am filled with gratitude and joy."

Reassessing the Positive Emotion:

After a round of tapping, the person reassesses their SUDS level for the positive emotion.

The goal is to see an increase in the SUDS level, indicating a rise in the intensity of the positive emotion.

Reinforcing the Positive State

The process can be repeated to further amplify the positive emotion or belief, using different affirmations or focusing on specific aspects of the desired state.

Benefits of Using SUDS to Enhance Positive Emotions:

Empowerment: By actively increasing positive emotions and beliefs, individuals can shift their focus from what they want to avoid to what they want to achieve or experience more of in their lives.

Balance and Well-Being: Elevating positive emotions helps balance out the energy system, contributing to overall emotional well-being and resilience.

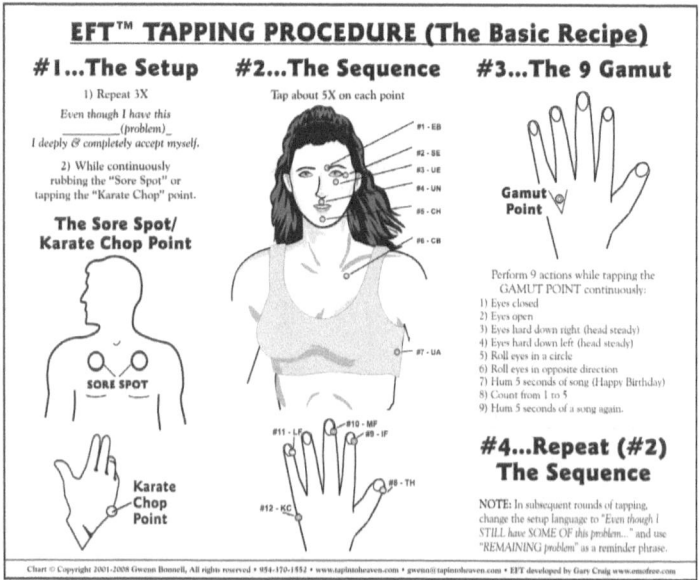

Reprogramming the Mind: Repeatedly tapping in positive statements can help reprogram the mind to default to these positive thoughts and emotions, making them more accessible in daily life.

Example Process

Step 1: Identify a positive goal: "I want to feel more confident in public speaking."

Step 2: Rate the current level of confidence on the SUDS scale (e.g., 4/10).

Step 3: Tap while saying, "I am becoming more confident every day," or "I speak with clarity and ease."

Step 4: Reassess the SUDS level for confidence (aiming for a higher score).

Step 5: Continue tapping until the desired positive emotion or belief reaches a 9 or 10 on the scale.

In this way, EFT tapping not only helps to reduce negative emotions but can also be a powerful tool for raising and solidifying positive emotional states, leading to a more balanced and empowered life.

Thymus Thump

The thymus gland, a powerful part of the body's energy system, can be tapped to release stuck emotions and restore balance. By tapping here, you can influence the energy flow in your body, especially when dealing with feelings of being unsafe or under attack. It wakes us up and is very influential in our immune system. . This is along your sternum , in the middle of your chest. tap up and down.

EFT Points and Emotional Connections

In EFT, each tapping point is associated with a body organ and, according to Chinese medicine, carries specific emotional energy. Below is a breakdown of the key tapping points, their corresponding meridians, and the emotions they are associated with:

1. Eyebrow (Bladder Meridian)

Emotion: Fear, insecurity, and holding on to the past.

Tapping here helps release: Feelings of fear or being overwhelmed, supporting a sense of security and calm.

2. Side of Eye (Gallbladder Meridian)

Emotion: Resentment, anger, and frustration.

Tapping here helps release: Anger and stress, promoting a clear vision and decision-making.

3. Under Eye (Stomach Meridian)

Emotion: Worry, anxiety, and feeling ungrounded.

Tapping here helps release: Excessive worry and anxiety, bringing calm and centering.

4. Under Nose (Governing Vessel)

Emotion: Guilt and shame.

Tapping here helps release: Guilt and shame, promoting self-acceptance and confidence.

5. Chin (Central Vessel)

Emotion: Confusion, embarrassment, and self-doubt.

Tapping here helps release: Feelings of unworthiness or self-doubt, encouraging clarity and self-assurance.

6. Collarbone (Kidney Meridian)

Emotion: Fear and feelings of insecurity.

Tapping here helps release: Deep-rooted fears, promoting security and courage.

7. Under Arm (Spleen Meridian)

Emotion: Lack of self-esteem, worry, and fear of rejection.

Tapping here helps release: Low self-worth and insecurity, boosting confidence and resilience.

8. Top of the Head (Governing Vessel)

Emotion: Spiritual disconnection and confusion.

Tapping here helps release: Mental and spiritual blockages, bringing clarity and connection to higher wisdom.

Under Breast (Liver Meridian): Anger, frustration, and unresolved emotional pain.

Gamut points

Thumb (Lung Meridian): Grief and sadness.

Index Finger (Large Intestine Meridian): Guilt and letting go.

Middle Finger (Circulation Meridian): Feeling stuck, unmotivated.

Baby Finger (Heart Meridian): Heartache, emotional pain.

Karate Point (Small Intestine Meridian): Fear of rejection, abandonment.

How to Integrate These Emotions into Your EFT Routine:

Identify the Emotion: Choose a specific emotion you are feeling or dealing with (e.g., anxiety, frustration).

The 9-Point Gamut Technique

The 9-Point Gamut is an additional technique within EFT that involves tapping a specific spot on the back of your hand while performing a series of actions that engage both hemispheres of the brain. This technique is particularly useful for processing deep emotional issues, releasing stress, and improving cognitive function by reprogramming old patterns and enhancing emotional flexibility.

The point you tap on during the 9-Point Gamut is located between the ring finger and the little finger on the back of the hand, in the depr

ession just above the knuckles. This point relates to the Triple Warmer Meridian, which is connected to the body's stress response and governs the fight-or-flight mechanism.

How the 9-Point Gamut Works Cognitively

When performing the 9-Point Gamut, you engage in a series of movements and actions that integrate the left and right brain hemispheres. These movements—such as eye shifts, humming, and counting—activate various parts of the brain, helping to release emotional blocks and rewire old neural pathways. This process works by breaking up habitual emotional responses and introducing cognitive flexibility, helping to process emotions more efficiently.

The Triple Warmer Meridian, when tapped during the Gamut process, is linked to the body's survival instincts. By calming the Triple Warmer, you reduce the fight-or-flight response, thereby reducing anxiety, stress, and emotional overwhelm.

9-Point Gamut Process

Find the Gamut Point- Locate the spot between the ring finger and the pinkie on the back of your hand.

Begin tapping this spot lightly but consistently.

Eyes closed - Eyes open

Eyes hard down to the right - Without moving your head,

look down to the right.

Eyes hard down to the left - Without moving your head, look down to the left.

Roll eyes in a circle - Slowly roll your eyes in a circle, clockwise.

Roll eyes in the opposite direction - Roll your eyes counterclockwise.

Hum a few seconds of a tune (this activates the right brain).

Count from 1 to 5 (this activates the left brain).

Hum again, a few more seconds of a tune.

This sequence integrates both hemispheres of the brain, helping to break through cognitive and emotional blocks, while tapping on the Triple Warmer calms the body's stress response.

Why These Movements Work

The eye movements, humming, and counting serve to stimulate different regions of the brain, allowing for a more comprehensive release of negative emotions. Here's a breakdown of how each action works

Eye Movements Stimulate the visual cortex and access different parts of the brain, similar to EMDR (Eye Movement Desensitization and Reprocessing), which is used to process trauma.

Humming Activates the creative and emotional centers of the brain, located in the right hemisphere.

Counting Engages the logical and analytical parts of the brain, located in the left hemisphere.

By integrating both sides of the brain, the Gamut sequence helps you to process emotional trauma or stress in a balanced, holistic way, promoting cognitive clarity and emotional resilience.

The Triple Warmer Meridian

The Triple Warmer (or Triple Burner) is responsible for regulating the body's autonomic response to stress. It acts as the body's alarm system, triggering the fight-or-flight response when we feel threatened. However, in modern life, this system can become overactive, causing chronic anxiety, fear, or stress. By tapping on the Gamut Point, you help calm the Triple Warmer, which in turn reduces the intensity of your stress response.

Incorporating the Gamut technique, especially when dealing with issues of anxiety, trauma, or deeply ingrained emotional patterns, enhances your tapping practice by allowing for a more comprehensive cognitive and emotional reset.

This week's tapping practice is all about deep cognitive and emotional transformation. With the Gamut technique, Triple Warmer, Sore points spots, and Thymus tapping you have more tools in your toolbox for transforming your life.

Way back then

"Healing is not about erasing the past, but about rewriting the story so it no longer defines you." – Unknown

I hadn't really gotten back to talking about what happened with my father. It's not that I fear it or hold any strong attachment to that event anymore. But revisiting the details doesn't feel necessary—not for you, and certainly not for me. Looking back at something that had such a deep impact, that created a ripple in my life, always carried with it the message that I wasn't enough. No matter what I did, I didn't fit in, I didn't belong, and nothing I ever did seemed to make me feel seen or worthy.

Growing up in that environment made me accustomed to surviving on scraps. Scraps of attention. Scraps of love. Scraps of validation. It wasn't just with my father; it became a pattern, one that I carried into my adult relationships. I was used to looking for those tiny moments of affection or kindness, holding onto them like they were lifelines, convincing myself that they meant more than they did. I once found myself in a relationship with a man who didn't treat me well—he drank too much, used drugs, and cheated. He was never truly there for me, not emotionally, not physically, not mentally. My children and I were left feeling less than, lost in the chaos of his neglect and cruelty. But I held on to the one small moment when he said something kind or the rare occasion when he cleared a plate from the table.

I took those moments and magnified them in my mind, telling myself that he had changed, that he cared, that he was the person I needed him to be. But that was never the reality. It was a one-sided conversation, with me doing all the talking, all the hoping, and all the believing. It's funny how we can cling to the smallest gestures when we're starving for love. When you've spent a lifetime feeling like you're not good enough, you start to settle for the bare minimum, believing it's all you deserve.

And then there's the piece of me that froze. I've heard of fight and flight—how we either run or confront the danger in front of us—but what I experienced was something different. It was freeze. That immobilizing sensation of being stuck, of not knowing where to go or what to do, because there was no escape, no safety, no place to hide. I was frozen in time, paralyzed in the moments when I needed to protect myself most. As a child, when my father's presence loomed large and there was no way to fight back or run away, I froze. My body may have been in the room, but my mind took me elsewhere. I escaped into a world of my own making, one where I could numb the pain and pretend that none of it was happening.

It wasn't until much later in life that I began to understand what that freeze response had done to me. There were entire periods of my childhood that I didn't remember, huge gaps in my memory where I had shut down completely. And in those frozen moments, I became an anxious child. It wasn't just an emotional or mental response—it became physical. I could never sit still. I'd flick my leg constantly, over and over, because the energy trapped inside me had no way out. My body was trying to release all the fear, all the uncertainty, all the pain, but I didn't know how to let it go.

That restlessness became a problem for my parents, particularly my mother. She couldn't understand why I was always fidgeting, why I could never be calm, why I was always seeking attention in the loudest, most desperate ways. But I wasn't doing it for attention—I was doing it because I didn't know how else to cope. I didn't know how to explain the anxiousness, the constant feeling of not being safe, not even in my own home.

The anxiety and the freeze response became two sides of the same coin. On one hand, I was constantly looking for a way out, always on edge, never comfortable where I was. On the other hand, I couldn't move, couldn't act, couldn't fight back. I was stuck in that moment, replaying the same feelings of fear and helplessness, over and over again.

Looking back now, I see how that frozen part of me affected so much of my life. I carried that anxiousness, that sense of never being safe, into every relationship, every interaction. And when I wasn't freezing, I was searching—searching for scraps of affection, searching for a place to belong, searching for someone who would tell me I was enough. But I was always looking outside of myself, hoping someone else would give me the validation I never got as a child.

It wasn't until I began to understand the depth of that freeze response, until I saw how it had shaped my entire worldview, that I began to heal. I started to see that the little girl who had frozen all those years ago was still waiting to feel safe, still waiting to be told she was enough. And it wasn't going to come from anyone else. It had to come from me.

and instead choose to see yourself in a new light, one of compassion, forgiveness, and power. I know that might sound overwhelming or even impossible when you're still stuck in the loop of feeling unworthy, but it's the only way to break free. You see, it wasn't about me not being good enough, it was about me not seeing that I was already enough. All the pain, all the searching for love in the wrong places, all the validation I chased—it was only because I didn't realize that I had it within me all along.

The anxiousness, the nervousness, the freeze that followed me through life, it was all part of the same story. A story where I had been conditioned to believe that love was something external, something I had to fight for or perform for, and if I didn't get it in the way I expected, it meant I wasn't worthy. But EFT tapping helped me break that story down. It allowed me to release the emotional imprint that my past had left on me—the imprint of not feeling safe, of feeling unloved, and of seeking validation in harmful ways.

There's something about tapping that creates space—space between the pain and the self, between the trauma and the present moment. And in that space, I found clarity. I realized that the sexual promiscuity wasn't about pleasure or desire—it was about validation, about thinking that if I gave my body, maybe I would receive love in return. But that love never came because it wasn't real. It was a stand-in, a placeholder for the self-love I hadn't yet cultivated.

I spent years waiting for someone else to make me feel worthy, always holding out hope that tomorrow would be better, that the next relationship would heal me, that someone would finally see me, and it would all make sense. But the truth is, no one else can fill those spaces within us. It's not their job. They can walk beside us, support us, even love us in beautiful ways, but they cannot fill the void that self-love was meant to fill.

And that's what I want you to understand now—self-love is not some abstract, distant concept. It's not about being perfect or always happy. It's about accepting yourself fully, flaws and all. It's about forgiving yourself for the times you didn't know better, for the times you stayed in relationships that hurt you, for the times you sought validation outside of yourself. It's about recognizing that the people who hurt you were hurt themselves, and that breaking that cycle starts with you.

So yes, self-love can be scary. It can feel like an impossible mountain to climb when you've spent your life believing you're not worthy. But it's the most important journey you'll ever take. Because once you start to love yourself, truly love yourself, everything changes. The relationships you attract, the way you respond to challenges, the way you see yourself in the mirror—it all begins to shift.

And I'm not saying it's easy. I'm not saying that the scars will disappear overnight. But I am saying that you have the power to start right now. To stop looking outside for what can only be found within. To stop blaming, stop feeling ashamed, stop living in the shadow of someone else's pain.

You get to rewrite the story. You get to decide that you are enough, that you've always been enough, and that your worth isn't dependent on anyone else's actions, approval, or love. You are here, right now, in this moment, with the opportunity to choose differently. To choose yourself.

And as you do, know that every step forward is a victory. Every time you choose self-love over self-doubt, you're rewriting the script not just for yourself, but for everyone who comes after you. The future generations, your children, your loved ones—they'll experience a new version of you, one that's whole, one that's healed, one that knows its worth. And that ripple effect? It's unstoppable.

So, I'm asking you now, as someone who's been in that place of darkness, as someone who's had to dig deep to find the light—make the choice. Choose self-love. Choose healing. Choose to see yourself as the magnificent being you've always been, even when the world tried to tell you otherwise. The time for blaming, shaming, and hiding is over. The time for you, for love, for wholeness, is now.

It's okay to acknowledge the ways we've lived and acted— they're part of our life, and we accept them. But starting today, let's do something that shows us what love really is. It won't just start with one thought, but with a commitment. I want to bring us back to the teachings of Louise Hay, who was instrumental in introducing the idea to Western culture that our thoughts create our reality. When I was going through some of my toughest times in the 2000s, I reached for her words, and I still do because they form the most beautiful, simple combination that can truly shift the balance.

The words are: "I love and approve of myself."

You might need to say these words 10 times, 100 times, or even 50,000 times—but saying them will turn the tide. We've spent years telling ourselves unimaginable negative things, millions of times. So, why is it surprising that we need to say something positive like "I love and approve of myself" just as often, if not more? I guarantee this: if you take nothing else from this book but this mantra, it will change your life. That's a promise. Your mind doesn't distinguish between good or bad thoughts—it just acts on the ones you repeat. If you keep saying, "I'm unlovable" or "I don't approve of myself," your life will reflect that belief. But if you say, consistently and persistently, "I love and approve of myself," your mind will act on that and create a new reality.

I feel deeply privileged to be writing this book, and I know it won't be my last. The next one is already taking shape. But for now, I would love to hear from you. What has shifted for you? What was your takeaway? Remember, we are all connected. Energy connects us in ways we may not always see. We are never truly alone, even though we may feel that way at times.

When we want to connect with others, the best way is by detaching from external validation and turning inward. Make this day the day you commit to yourself. You've made promises to others—your parents, your boss, your friends, and even strangers. You've given them your energy, your time, your hard work. But today, I'm asking you to make a commitment to you. Say it with me: "I love and approve of myself."

Say it as many times as you can over the next week. Say it hundreds, thousands of times. Then do it for another week, and another. Keep saying it for seven weeks, and then seven months. Watch as your life begins to shift.

This is your moment.
You are worth this effort. Let's do it together

From the mighty and marvelous —Louis. L. Hay

In the infinity of life where I am
All is perfect, whole, and complete
I support myself, and life supports me
I see evidence of the Law working all around me
And in every area of my life
I reinforce that which I learn in joyous ways
My day begins with gratitude and joy
I look forward with enthusiasm to the adventures of the day
Knowing that in my life "All is good"
I love who I am and all that I do
I am the living, loving, joyous expression of life
All is well in my world.

We have to remember that as we move through life, especially after doing deep work, it's easy to feel like we're done once we've cleared away some of the emotional baggage. I know this firsthand because I experienced it myself. After going through counseling, learning EFT, and working on myself, I thought I could just move forward and live happily. But then came the hiccup—the realization that I hadn't fully integrated daily habits that supported continued growth and creation. I had let go of a lot, but I wasn't yet grounded in the daily actions that would truly move me forward.

I learned that small habits and small steps add up over time. It's not just about clearing the past; it's about what we do in the present that propels us into the future. I wasn't using my daily time to stay in that flow of creation, that slipstream where things come together and we feel aligned. I had to learn this lesson: life is not static. We're always moving, either upward or downward. If we're not actively nourishing our mind with positive thoughts, we can easily slip back into old patterns. Our mind doesn't differentiate between good or bad thoughts—it simply acts on the ones we feed it.

This is where daily habits come into play. We have absolute power over our thoughts, and we are the only ones who can change them. If we're constantly stressed about others, we're giving them power over us. They didn't take it; we gave it to them. That realization is profound. So, what we do each day matters immensely. How do you think about yourself? What emotions are priming your day? Are you connecting to your body, your lifelong companion? These habits don't just shape your mindset; they also shape your health. When you align your thoughts and actions with self-love and self-care, everything begins to shift.

Our health is our true wealth, which is our mind, body, and soul. The richness of life comes from being connected to the present moment, to the world around us, and to ourselves. Your habits create you, and they start with your thoughts. After you've done all the work outlined in this book, especially when you reach that pivotal moment—represented by cup 5—you'll find that you have a choice. Life is a continuous process of creation. I know it can feel daunting to think, "Do I really have to keep doing this?" But it's not about doing it because you have to; it's about becoming someone who naturally embodies these practices. When it no longer feels like a chore, that's when you know you've reached a new level of self-acceptance and self-approval.

So, as you clear out the old, make sure you're filling that space with things that matter, with habits that will shape the version of yourself you're becoming. This is lifelong work, but it's also the most rewarding work you'll ever do.

Fight, Flight, Freeze and Fawn

Let's dive into the details of each response, including Fight, Flight, Freeze, and Fawn, and how they manifest in the body and mind.

1. Fight Response

The fight response is the impulse to confront a threat head-on. This is the body's way of preparing to defend itself, often with aggression or assertiveness. When someone perceives they have enough power to fight off a threat, this response kicks in.

What Happens in the Body During Fight

Sympathetic Nervous System Activation: The fight response is driven by the activation of the sympathetic nervous system, which ramps up the body's physical abilities.

Increased Heart Rate: The heart pumps faster to deliver oxygen-rich blood to muscles, preparing them for intense physical action.

Adrenaline Surge: The release of adrenaline fuels the body's energy, boosting alertness, muscle strength, and speed.

Muscle Tension: Muscles tense up, often creating sensations of strength or readiness for combat. This can lead to clenched fists, a tightened jaw, or a rigid posture.

Psychological Experience of Fight:

Anger and Aggression: The fight response is often accompanied by anger or irritation. This emotion provides the mental push to engage with or confront the threat.

Confrontation: The person may feel an urge to argue, lash out, or physically fight. They feel a heightened sense of control over the situation and might become verbally or physically aggressive to overcome the perceived danger.

Hyperfocus on the Threat: The brain hones in on the perceived danger, heightening awareness of the threat while ignoring non-essential details.

When Fight Becomes Harmful:

While the fight response is valuable in situations of true physical danger, it can be destructive when triggered unnecessarily. For instance, it can manifest as hostility in relationships, impatience, or even violence in situations where cooperation or calmness would serve better.

2. Flight Response

The flight response is the instinct to escape from danger. In this state, the body is prepared for rapid movement and evasion. This response typically arises when the individual feels that running away is the safest option.

What Happens in the Body During Flight:

Sympathetic Nervous System Activation: Similar to the fight response, the sympathetic nervous system readies the body for fast, evasive action.

Increased Heart Rate and Breathing: The heart beats faster, and breathing becomes more rapid to deliver more oxygen to muscles.

Hypervigilance: The mind becomes acutely aware of escape routes, possible dangers, and anything that might hinder a successful flight. Eyes might dart around the environment.

Muscle Readiness: Muscles, especially in the legs, prepare for quick action. This can manifest as a jittery feeling or an urge to run.

Psychological Experience of Flight:

Anxiety and Panic: The person may feel an overwhelming sense of fear or panic, driving them to seek immediate escape.

Restlessness: There may be an inability to stay still, with constant movement or pacing as the mind tries to find ways to avoid the perceived danger.

Avoidance: The individual might avoid people, situations, or responsibilities that feel overwhelming or threatening, whether that threat is real or imagined.

When Flight Becomes Harmful:

The flight response, while useful in the presence of physical danger, can lead to chronic avoidance in everyday life. People might avoid conflict, difficult emotions, or even positive challenges. In extreme cases, this can result in social isolation or phobias, as the person becomes increasingly focused on evasion rather than engagement.

3. Freeze Response

The freeze response occurs when neither fight nor flight seem like viable options. The body becomes immobile, which can manifest as feeling "frozen," paralyzed, or numb. This response often kicks in when escape or defense seems impossible, and the body opts to "play dead" to avoid further harm.

What Happens in the Body During Freeze:

Parasympathetic Nervous System Activation: The freeze response involves the parasympathetic nervous system, leading to a drop in energy, heart rate, and breathing. This contrasts with the high energy of fight or flight.

Muscle Paralysis or Tension: While in freeze, muscles may become stiff and tense, but there is no release of that energy. The person may feel physically immobilized, stuck, or like they can't move or speak.

Numbness or Detachment: A person may feel disconnected from their body or surroundings, experiencing a sense of emotional or physical numbness. This is often a coping mechanism to shield against trauma or overwhelming stress.

Psychological Experience of Freeze:

Dissociation: The freeze response is closely linked with dissociation, where a person mentally "checks out" to protect themselves from overwhelming emotions or sensations. This can make time feel distorted or unreal.

Feeling Stuck: The individual may experience intense helplessness or a feeling of being trapped, both physically and mentally.

Shame and Self-Blame: Many people who experience the freeze response, especially trauma survivors, feel guilt or shame afterward because they did not take action. This can compound their emotional distress, even though the freeze response is an automatic, unconscious survival mechanism.

4. Fawn Response

The fawn response was introduced by Pete Walker to describe the behavior of appeasing or placating others to avoid conflict or harm. This response is often seen in individuals who have experienced chronic or complex trauma, where the safest survival strategy is to please the threat.

What Happens in the Body During Fawn:

Sympathetic Nervous System Activation: The body is still in a state of high alert, but instead of fighting or fleeing, the individual directs their energy toward appeasing the source of stress or danger.

Stress Hormones: Cortisol and adrenaline may still be present, but instead of preparing for action, the body focuses on placating the perceived threat.

Hypervigilance Toward Others: The person becomes highly attuned to the emotions and needs of others, often to the point of neglecting their own feelings and boundaries.

Psychological Experience of Fawn:

People-Pleasing: The person may exhibit behaviors designed to keep others happy, even if it means sacrificing their own needs or desires. This can include agreeing to things they don't want, avoiding confrontation, or going to great lengths to avoid making others upset.

Loss of Identity: Over time, the fawn response can lead to a loss of self-identity, as the individual becomes so focused on others that they forget their own values, desires, or boundaries.

Codependency: Individuals may form unhealthy relationships where they rely on pleasing others for their sense of safety or self-worth.

When Fawn Becomes Harmful: While fawning can help avoid immediate danger in abusive or high-conflict situations, over time, it can lead to codependency, burnout, and an erosion of self-esteem. Individuals may struggle to assert their needs or feel empowered to make decisions, always deferring to others' desires.

The fight, flight, freeze, and fawn responses are all natural survival mechanisms, each playing a crucial role in how we respond to perceived threats. However, when these responses become chronic or habitual, especially due to past trauma, they can hinder rather than help us. Recognizing these responses is the first step in regaining control, allowing individuals to shift from survival mode to a more empowered and balanced way of living.

Hiccups Along the Way

Even though the new beliefs feel empowering, when faced with a challenging decision, you might revert to indecision or procrastination because those behaviors feel safer. The brain craves predictability, and change—even positive change—can feel uncomfortable.

You may find yourself second-guessing your choices again or fearing that you'll fail, which brings back the old narratives of "I can't trust myself" or "I'm not capable."

Without being consistent, the old limiting beliefs may resurface because the internal work hasn't fully solidified. For example, you may stop reinforcing positive self-talk or avoid taking courageous actions, slipping back into fear of failure or procrastination.

To stay in the flow of these new, positive beliefs, you need continuous nurturing and self-awareness.

It's inevitable that setbacks will occur. The key is not to let a slip become a spiral. When you notice yourself reverting to old patterns, practice self-compassion rather than harsh judgment. Acknowledge that progress isn't linear and that each step back is an opportunity to learn and reinforce your growth.

Achieving lasting change requires ongoing attention and consistent action. Slipping back into old patterns is a natural part of the process, but with awareness and tools, you can recover more quickly and continue to move forward. Recognizing these potential hiccups and maintaining a mindset of curiosity and compassion toward yourself will keep you on track toward the life you're creating.

By staying present, acknowledging when you're veering off course, and regularly engaging in practices that reinforce your new beliefs, you'll remain forward-moving and confident in your ability to create the life you want.

We are, after all, Human

Humans have two distinct capacities. One is the capacity to hesitate, which has stopped many of us from following our dreams and moving forward. When we hesitate, we often get stuck in our heads, unable to make decisions. We go round and round, and that hesitation costs us dearly. It costs us creativity, time, and momentum. It also stops us from being where we are meant to be. Often, that place where we could be is exactly where we're meant to be, but we hold ourselves back, trapped in hesitation.

The second capacity is an imbalanced, exaggerated need to suffer. Suffering has become glorified in our culture, with ideas like "no pain, no gain" dominating the way we think about hard work, especially in the gym. The idea that you must push, stretch, and exhaust yourself is common. Yes, when you're physically training, there is a level of discomfort involved to achieve results. But if the goal is to suffer, you're sending a message to yourself, to your body, and to your emotions that nothing good can come into your life unless you suffer first.

Suffering creates a future-focused mindset, always looking ahead to some goal that will supposedly bring happiness. How many times have we told ourselves, "When I achieve this, then I'll be happy"? This mentality keeps us in a cycle where happiness is always a future event, never something we experience in the present. We drag ourselves toward a goal that never seems to arrive. The outcome we are waiting for never manifests because we are too focused on the suffering it takes to get there.

This is where we need to ask ourselves: how many places in life do we believe suffering is necessary? Consider relationships. In how many ways do you feel that you must endure suffering to achieve something good? You might endure uncomfortable conversations or suppress your own needs so that your partner's opinions seem more important than yours. That silence is a form of suffering, one that overlaps with codependency, people-pleasing, and feelings of inadequacy. We believe suffering is inevitable in these situations, but it doesn't have to be.

Suffering has become intertwined with the idea of hard work, but they are not the same. Working hard toward something meaningful and pleasurable brings a sense of purpose and energy that connects you to yourself, the universe, and everyone around you. Hard work can create great feelings of accomplishment, but that doesn't mean it must involve suffering. Suffering only becomes part of hard work if we make it so.

Now think about your career, your work, or your calling. Is it causing suffering? Is it pushing you in ways that disconnect you from your joy? Is it telling you that you don't have time for family, for self-care, for rest? These are signs that the narrative of suffering has become attached to your work. But success doesn't have to come at the cost of your well-being.

It's important to understand that rushing, pushing, and suffering toward a goal isn't the only way. There's another path, one that doesn't involve sacrifice but instead embraces joy, presence, and alignment with purpose. There are people who believe you can't have it all, but others believe you can. Life is made up of many areas, and balance is possible without the need for suffering.

Hesitation and suffering are deeply ingrained in how we approach life, but they don't need to be. By recognizing these patterns, we can begin to reshape our experience and move forward with clarity, joy, and ease.

It is about the journey. It is about you being on the journey. So how many places in your life do you have a belief that you must suffer? Let's break this down in relationships. How often do you think that you must do, have, or be something from a place of suffering to get what you think is something good? You put up with conversations. You might try to be a certain way just to keep some benefit coming in. You might feel like you have to suffer through not being able to enjoy a meal out or indulge in something you enjoy. You might even go against your own opinions, giving more weight to your partner's thoughts than your own. This silence is suffering.

It often crosses into codependency, people-pleasing, and not feeling good enough. Suffering, in combination with codependency, feels as if it is in our water. It flows through every aspect of our lives. There's this notion that suffering is necessary. But working hard doesn't necessarily mean suffering. Working hard towards something that is purposeful and brings pleasure creates an amazing energetic momentum. You connect with yourself, the universe, and everything around you. The feeling of accomplishment is intrinsic. It's not just about reaching the goal, but about the feelings you cultivate along the way. Suffering does not have to be part of that journey—unless you choose to make it so.

Now think about your career, your work, or your calling. Are you suffering in it? Is it pushing you in negative directions? Are you telling yourself that you don't have time for family, that you can't take care of your body, all in the name of some future goal? But it's not about rushing, is it?

There's a woman named Reagan Hillier from New Zealand, who shared a quote from Oprah Winfrey, saying you can't have it all. But Reagan disagrees, and so do I. She believes, and I believe, that you can have it all. I work out of nine areas of life, and I am writing a book about this, called Eight Baskets in a Trolley. It will be out in 2025, and it's going to dive deep into these areas, showing how we can change our narratives. How we can remove the suffering and start creating something wonderful.

Do you suffer when it comes to your health? What about your relationship with money? Do you believe that you can't have money or that you must hold on to it tightly, never allowing yourself to spend?

There's a man named Ken Honda who wrote Happy Money. He speaks about surrendering to the flow and having a conversation with money in a positive, powerful way. It's not about suffering. His ideas can shift how you think about money. And then there is Mr. Hicks, who teaches about the vibrational energy we all possess. If you rub your hands together quickly for sixty seconds and then slowly pull them apart, you can feel the energy. We are all energetic beings, and everything in our life is connected through energy.

When we feel stuck and surrounded by negative thoughts, it's a reflection of how unsafe we feel in our own bodies. Years ago, I had a fear that if I traveled to another country, there wouldn't be any air for me to breathe. It was an irrational fear, of course, but it was trapped in my mind. That fear is gone now, but back then, it was suffocating.

We have to remember that life does not have to be a struggle. That belief is a construct of society, designed to keep us stuck. There are enough resources for everyone. I'll admit that I used to struggle with the messages from Esther Hicks. They grated on me. It wasn't her message—it was that I wasn't vibrating at the right place to receive it. I hadn't shifted out of my own limiting beliefs. Hicks talks about flow and ease, about not forcing yourself to suffer.

We often create our own suffering because we believe it's the only way to achieve something good. But think about it—if you're doing things for the sake of doing them, without any good coming from them, what's the point? We are also denying our own happiness, pushing it away, thinking we don't deserve to feel good while moving forward.

We beat ourselves up for all the wrong reasons. We haven't spent enough time affirming our worth, saying, "I love myself. I am enough. I am loving, lovable, and loved." Instead, we let the negative voices take over. We measure ourselves by other people's standards, by society's narrative that tells us we aren't doing enough. It tells us that our worth is in our doing, in how much we produce. But this direction leads to a tipping point—a tipping point that pulls us downward.

The more we chase validation through struggle, the more life feels like it's working against us. We keep thinking that if we just get to the next step, we'll be enough, but it's never enough. We have to struggle more.

This belief system is what keeps us trapped in suffering. It keeps us overthinking, worrying, and hesitating. But remember, if we're wringing our hands, we can't roll up our sleeves. Worry, overthinking, and hesitation keep us stuck.

So, take action in the moment. If you have a thought, write it down. Keep a notebook by your bed so you can release these thoughts and let them go.

There are two things you can do before going to bed. First, you can write a list of 10 things you're grateful for. Or, you can ask yourself empowering questions like, "How can I be better tomorrow? What can I do to make myself feel better? How do I want to feel tomorrow, and how do I see my life going?"

Alternatively, you can read five to 10 pages of a self-help book that will move you forward. The key is to ensure the last thing on your mind before you sleep is positive. Even if you've been worrying, you're intentionally inputting positive energy into your mind beforehand. You might be thankful for simple things—the bed you're sleeping in, a conversation you had, the meal you ate, or even the fact that your body helped you move through the day. You could be grateful for your children, partner, parents, or friends, or for a moment of relaxation, a walk, or watching your favorite program.

When you do this—writing down your gratitude list or reading from a helpful book—you are creating a new vibrational imprint for your subconscious to work on while you sleep. This process primes your energy for the next day. The hours between when you fall asleep and when you wake up become a time of transformation because you've set yourself up with new information and positive thoughts. When you wake up, your mind is already in a positive frame, and you're ready to prime your day with good energy.

Now, imagine doing this consistently for 21 days. How long will it be before you notice a shift in your mindset, before you wake up with encouraging thoughts, or before you feel more gratitude for your body, which in turn responds better to you? How long before you experience less stress, less overthinking, and less worry? It might take just those 21 days, the time it takes to begin rewiring your brain. Remember, habits aren't hard-wired into us. Negative thinking, smoking, any unhelpful habit—all of these can be changed. When we introduce new information, our brain starts to fire new connections, new sparks of ideas, and build new ways of being.

You have the habit, and the habit has you. But when you change your habits, you begin to change your life. Throughout the day, between morning and night, you'll notice new ways of coping with life's challenges. Instead of reacting, you'll start responding. You'll give yourself the emotional and mental space to pause and breathe. You might even find yourself doing box breathing at lunchtime after an uncomfortable conversation, or stretching your body because you recognize that changing your physical posture helps you shift your mindset. By doing so, you'll start showing up differently, more empowered and grounded.

Hesitation is a human thing that often stops us, but action propels us forward. Write things down when they come to you—keep a notebook by your bed or use a memo app on your phone to capture your thoughts. Honor the ideas and insights that flow through your subconscious and superconscious mind. Our conscious mind is limited in scope, but when we allow our subconscious and superconscious to filter insights into our awareness, it's like experiencing little epiphanies. Clarity, perspective, and a sense of wonder return to our lives.

Rather than struggling, we become curious. And curiosity, combined with learning and engagement with the world, opens us up to emotions we thought we couldn't feel—joy, fulfillment, satisfaction, purpose, and connection. All these things become tangible, and the vibrancy of life grows. Suddenly, life begins to change, and you realize that there truly is enough for everyone. The resources, the opportunities, and the energy—there is enough for all of us.

You will be able to navigate the situation with calmness and clarity. Trusting yourself is about building that internal confidence, knowing that in each moment, you are equipped to handle whatever comes your way. This doesn't mean you have all the answers ahead of time, but it does mean that you have faith in your ability to figure it out when the time comes.

When anxiety creeps in, it's often because we are trying to control outcomes or predict the future. But trust allows us to step back from that need for control and embrace the present moment with openness. Anxiety thrives on the unknown, but trust thrives on the belief that whatever happens, you'll manage.

Start small by making daily choices where you reinforce trust. Maybe you decide not to plan every interaction down to the last detail, allowing for some spontaneity and space to respond naturally. Maybe you let go of the habit of rehearsing difficult conversations in your head and instead affirm that when the time comes, you will know what to say. Each time you do this, you strengthen your trust muscles, making it easier to live from a place of inner peace.

As you practice this, you'll notice that anxiety begins to lose its grip. You'll start to feel more in control—not because you've meticulously planned everything out, but because you've built trust in yourself to handle things as they come. You'll begin to see that life doesn't have to be about constantly reacting to every situation with fear or stress. Instead, it can be about responding thoughtfully, trusting that the right answers will come, and feeling more grounded and present.

Trust shifts the focus from external circumstances, which are often unpredictable, to your own inner resources, which are always available. When you operate from trust, you begin to notice a sense of calm, even in the face of uncertainty. You stop feeling like you need to control every aspect of your life, and instead, you flow with it. This doesn't mean you won't ever feel fear or anxiety again, but it means those feelings won't dictate your actions.

The beautiful thing about trust is that it creates space for curiosity and learning. When you trust yourself, you're more willing to take risks, explore new opportunities, and engage with life in a more vibrant way. You start to see challenges as opportunities for growth rather than threats to your well-being. This shift in perspective allows you to live a more fulfilling and joyful life, one where anxiety takes a backseat, and trust leads the way.

So, how do you build this trust? It starts with small, consistent actions—affirmations, mindfulness, and self-reflection. Ask yourself each day, "How can I trust myself more today?" and take note of the moments where you allow trust to guide your decisions. Over time, you'll begin to see a transformation in how you handle life's ups and downs. Trust becomes your anchor, and with it, anxiety begins to dissolve, making space for peace, clarity, and confidence.

Stop looking for happiness in the same place you lost it.
—Paulo Coelho

Anxiety is a huge, widespread pandemic in our society today. Everyone has experienced some form of it, as it's a natural part of our body's response to excitement. Interestingly, excitement and anxiety stem from the same place within us. But more often than not, we misinterpret the energy of something new as anxiety, mainly because we are fearful. Fear creates anxiety—fear of whether we can handle things, fear of whether we will cope with what's ahead. I've been there, and you might be there now or have been before, where you feel the need to organize everything in your mind to somehow manage what's coming. You try to line up all the ducks, thinking, "If this happens, then that can happen, and then I'll cope." But that planning takes you out of the present moment, as your mind races, trying to figure out all the possibilities and outcomes. And where are you? You're no longer here. You're somewhere else entirely—lost in that place of fear. Anxiety is the opposite of trust.

Now, let's talk about trust—the most incredible ingredient for creating the best recipe for your life. When we can trust ourselves to be safe, we also trust that the decisions we make will be the right ones. You may have heard me speak about affirmations and power statements, about changing what we say to ourselves. But today, I feel this topic of trust deserves its own conversation because it's fundamental to living the life you want.

When we trust ourselves, we no longer rely solely on our thoughts and overactive minds. We begin to feel. Instead of saying, "I think that will happen," we learn to tune into our bodies and say, "I feel..." This shift is key because our bodies hold a different kind of wisdom. Our body has its own mind. Dr Joe Dispenza talks about this beautifully in his work—how our bodies hold memories, patterns, and intelligence. This isn't a new concept, but people are starting to take action on it now. The difference between knowing something and acting on it is where transformation lies.

So much of what we talk about—whether it's trust, anxiety, or building new habits—has been around for a long time. But sometimes, we aren't ready to receive the message. It's like that old proverb, "When the student is ready, the teacher will appear." When you're in the right place, suddenly things you hadn't noticed before will start making sense. You begin to hear, feel, and know truths that have been waiting for you all along.

Building trust in ourselves requires us to strengthen our internal muscles. This is where we create a container—a space to hold the new beliefs, the new feelings, and the new thoughts we want to cultivate. It's like a cup of tea: thoughts, emotions, and actions blend to create a new flow in our lives. And it's up to you—what kind of tea will you have today?

When we can say, "I trust myself to be okay no matter what comes," something amazing happens. You begin to feel confident that, in the moment when it matters, you will have all the information and tools you need to make the right decision. You don't have to figure it all out now. But many people are already trying to solve future problems, mentally rehearsing conversations, or worrying about outcomes that haven't happened yet. This creates fear, and that fear fuels anxiety. Instead, if you shift your thinking to trusting yourself in the moment, you ease that anxiety.

Many of us spend hours after a disagreement, for example, thinking about what we should have said, or planning what we'll say next time. We rehearse conversations in our heads, trying to control future interactions. And while we do this, we experience all the emotions—anger, frustration, fear—right here in the present. Our bodies don't know the difference. They're feeling these emotions now as though the event is happening, and it drains us. This mental rehearsal of fear is creating anxiety, instead of trusting that when the moment comes, we will know what to say or do.

Trusting yourself to make the best decision in the moment is a key to better living.

Igniting Your Own Fire

Nobody else is responsible for getting me up in the morning, for getting me to focus, for driving me forward. That is my job. If I want a bigger, better life, I have to show up for it. I have to be the one to strike the match, to light my own fire. When that flame burns bright enough, then, and only then, will I attract the people, opportunities, and resources to fan it into something greater. But it starts with me. I am the spark. Just as you are the spark.

If I don't feed my fire, it will die. I cannot rely on anyone else to keep it burning. It's not someone else's job to ignite my passion, my drive, or my ambition. That responsibility lies within me. And the same is true for you.

Every single day, you have a choice. You can lie in bed, stagnant and waiting, or you can choose to rise. You can choose to move toward the life you dream of. But waiting for someone else to save you or push you forward is a dead end. No one is coming to hand you this life on a silver platter. You are the one who must take daily actions, make bold decisions, and stay consistent in fueling your fire.

Start being the person you want to be. Dress the part, think the part, live the part—right now. You don't need to wait for everything to be perfect. If resources are limited, there's always a way. It is definitely through a small, intentional change in your daily habits, it's about your choices. Every choice either adds fuel to your fire or smothers it.

When those negative thoughts creep in, as they inevitably will, you have to be vigilant. Replace each one with three positive thoughts. Interrupt your own patterns. Because nobody is going to do it for you. Your dream life is waiting around the corner, you can decide to walk there.

So, what have you done today to light your fire? What steps have you taken to keep it burning strong? Are you feeding your own flame, or are you letting it fizzle out?

Every single day, I go all in. I'm relentless about filling my cup, feeding my fire, and nurturing the things that matter to me. I've gotten hungry for my dreams, determined to make them a reality. And I believe—deep in my soul—that it's all there waiting for me. The life I want is there for me to claim. And it's there for you, too.

But it's up to you to strike the match.

Time to say goodbye for now

Together, we have traveled a remarkable journey of self-exploration, growth, and transformation. From the muddy puddles of life's challenges to the bright light of personal awakening, you have ignited something powerful within yourself. Through these chapters, we've uncovered valuable insights, explored new perspectives, and discovered practical tools designed to help you evolve into the best version of yourself.

At the heart of this journey is a simple but profound truth: everything begins and ends with you. Your thoughts, actions, and beliefs shape the world around you. You matter—just as the next person does—not from a place of ego, but from an awareness that the way we respond to life determines how we experience it. When we recognize this, we can make conscious choices that align with our highest selves, creating a life filled with purpose and connection.

A vital tool introduced in this book is EFT tapping, a tremendous resource for personal healing and growth. EFT (Emotional Freedom Techniques) empowers you to release stuck emotions, reframe limiting beliefs, and reduce the emotional impact of past experiences. By gently tapping on specific points on your body, you can calm your nervous system, rewire emotional responses, and restore balance.

It is a simple yet transformative practice that you can use throughout your life to manage stress, process emotions, and maintain inner peace.

The core of this book is about giving you tools, like EFT tapping, to help you unlock your potential, regulate emotions, and build the version of you that you like and love. It all starts with self-awareness, self-compassion, and a willingness to grow.

Healing is about integrating all parts of yourself—embracing your light and shadow.

As you grow, you shine your light for others to see, contributing meaningfully to the world around you. Living with purpose and joy becomes natural when you are in alignment with your true self.

As you close this book, acknowledge the work you've done and the tools you've gained, like EFT tapping, that will support you throughout life. This journey is ongoing, but with the insights and skills you've cultivated, you're better equipped to live a purposeful, joy-filled life. You've taken action today—be proud of that. Your story matters, and the tools you've gained will help you continue to write it in powerful and positive ways. Keep moving forward, and remember, you are worthy of all the light and joy life has to offer.

This is your journey, and every step has brought you closer to a fuller, richer understanding of who you truly are and the limitless potential that lies within you.

Kindest Thoughts and Good Fortune to you all,

Elysabeth Wolter

Resources and what next

Recommendations

Here is a list of people that you may want to investigate further. I have given you a wide range of choices. Enjoy

Louise Hay: You Can Heal Your Life and Others: Hay's work emphasizes the power of self-love and affirmations to transform one's life by healing emotional wounds and negative thinking.

Susan Jeffers: Feel the Fear and Do It Anyway: Susan Jeffers' teachings helped you make important life changes, focusing on overcoming fear and empowering oneself through action.

Vishen Lakhiani: 'The Code of the Extraordinary Mind. Founder of Mindvalley, Lakhiani combines personal development and spiritual growth. His programs and free masterclasses emphasize emotional intelligence, body wellness, and personal development.

Tim Storey: An insightful perspective on personal growth, offering spiritual and emotional healing tools.

Julia Cameron: The Artist's Way: A Seminal Guide for Creative Recovery, and also many more books, including "Your Right to Write'

Dr. Joe Dispenza – 'You Are the Placebo',' Breaking the Habit of Being Yourself and others plus workshops/retreats. He blends neuroscience and meditation, helping ordinary people achieve extraordinary results.

Dr. Bruce Lipton: The Biology of Belief: Known for his work on epigenetics, Lipton explores how beliefs influence biology and health.

Tony Robbins: Renowned for his motivational speaking and transformative courses in personal development and wealth-building.

Tim Ferris: The 4-Hour Workweek and The 4-Hour Body: Ferris focuses on optimizing time and energy for both professional and personal development.

Brandon Bays: The Journey: An inspiring method for emotional and spiritual healing.

Paulo Coelho: The Alchemist: A spiritual allegory about following one's personal legend.

Joseph Murphy: The Power of Your Subconscious Mind: An older book with timeless wisdom on harnessing the subconscious to manifest desired outcomes.

Gabrielle Roth: Known for her work on movement and embodiment as a healing modality.

Andrew Huberman's Podcast: Focuses on neuroscience, performance, and health optimization—offering practical advice on how our brain and body can work in harmony.

Esther Hicks & Abraham's Teachings: Known for the Law of Attraction and channeled messages from Abraham, Esther Hicks provides tools for manifesting desires by aligning energy with well-being and abundance. Her work, including Ask and It Is Given, is foundational in teaching people how to consciously create their reality through vibration and positive thinking.

Joe Vitale: Featured in The Secret, Vitale focuses on the Law of Attraction as well, but with an emphasis on clearing subconscious blocks to attract wealth and success. His book The Attractor Factor is a popular read, and his teachings often merge spirituality with marketing and success principles.

Rhonda Byrne: Best known for her groundbreaking book The Secret, Byrne helped bring the Law of Attraction to the mainstream. Her work has expanded into books like The Power and The Magic, further deepening the exploration of how our thoughts create our reality.

Paul McKenna: Known for his self-help books and audio programs, McKenna focuses on personal transformation through hypnosis and neuro-linguistic programming (NLP). His works like I Can Make You Thin and Change Your Life in 7 Days offer practical tools for overcoming bad habits, weight loss, confidence building, and achieving success through subconscious reprogramming.

Ken Honda: The Money Man: Known as Japan's zen millionaire, Ken Honda blends financial wisdom with emotional well-being in his book Happy Money. His teachings focus on creating a healthy, peaceful relationship with money, emphasizing gratitude, flow, and a giving mindset rather than fear or scarcity.

Denise Duffield-Thomas: Is a money mindset mentor and author known for helping entrepreneurs and individuals break free from limiting beliefs about wealth and financial success. Her work often focuses on clearing the mental and emotional blocks that prevent people from achieving financial abundance. Denise's style combines practical advice with insights on how mindset can impact one's relationship with money. Her message often emphasizes ease and flow in manifesting wealth rather than hustling or overworking.

Jen Sincero- a motivational speaker and bestselling author known for her sassy, humorous approach to self-help and personal development. Her books encourage readers to embrace a mindset of positivity, confidence, and abundance, often with an emphasis on overcoming self-doubt and taking action. Jen's work is infused with a bold, irreverent tone that resonates with those looking for a more casual, yet impactful, approach to personal growth.

Brad Yates: Approach: Brad Yates is known for his accessible, light-hearted, and practical approach to EFT tapping. His YouTube channel is filled with hundreds of EFT videos covering a variety of issues, from emotional blockages to success and self-improvement.

YouTube Channel: One of the most extensive free EFT video libraries online.

Nick Ortner & Jessica Ortner: Nick Ortner is a leading figure in the modern EFT movement, known for bringing EFT to the mainstream with a focus on stress, health, and overall well-being. He is the founder of The Tapping Solution. Jessica Ortner, Nick's sister, focuses on the application of EFT for women, particularly in areas of body confidence and weight loss.

Gary Craig is the original creator of EFT and pioneered the use of tapping techniques to clear emotional blocks and reduce psychological stress.

EmoFree.com: Gary Craig's official website that includes many free resources, articles, and case studies on EFT.

Donna Eden & David Feinstein: Donna Eden is a pioneer in the field of energy medicine, with decades of experience teaching people to work with their body's energy systems for self-healing.

Energy Medicine: This book is a comprehensive guide to working with the body's energy systems to boost health and vitality. It offers practical techniques for maintaining emotional balance, strengthening the immune system, and relieving pain.

David Feinstein is a clinical psychologist who works alongside Donna Eden, integrating traditional psychology with energy healing techniques. He is known for his work in energy psychology.

"It's strange that we live in a culture that tells us not to be a "Pollyanna" What's wrong with feeling good about life despite what obstacles come our way? What's wrong with looking at the sun instead of doom and gloom? What's wrong with trying to say good and old things? NOTHING IS WRONG WITH IT! Why would you want to think any other way?" —Susan Jeffers

"If I must be faithful to someone or something, I must first of all, be faithful to myself." —Paul Coelho

My contacts

Website: www.lizziesinsights.co.nz

Join the free Facebook tapping group here

https://www.facebook.com/groups/turnthetidewithtapping

My main Facebook page and Lizzies Insights page

https://www.facebook.com/elysabeth.wolterartist

https://www.facebook.com/lizzieinsights/

https://www.instagram.com/

https://www.youtube.com/@lizzieinsights5857

https://www.tiktok.com/@lizzies.insights

Email: lizziesinsights@gmail.com

Watch out for The Fairy Elephant Effect Podcast

www.ingramcontent.com/pod-product-compliance
Lightning Source LLC
Chambersburg PA
CBHW031246290426
44109CB00012B/458